THEATRES OF CONSCIENCE
1939–53

Routledge Harwood Contemporary Theatre Studies
A series of books edited by Franc Chamberlain, University College
Northampton, UK

**Please see the back of this book for other titles in the Contemporary Theatre
Studies series**

THEATRES OF CONSCIENCE 1939–53

A STUDY OF FOUR TOURING BRITISH COMMUNITY THEATRES

Peter Billingham
Bath Spa University College
Bath, UK

ROUTLEDGE
Taylor & Francis Group

London and New York

First published 2002
by Routledge
11 New Fetter Lane, London EC4P 4EE

Simultaneously published in the USA and Canada
by Routledge
29 West 35th Street, New York 10001

Routledge is an imprint of the Taylor & Francis Group

© 2002 Taylor & Francis

Typeset by Scientifik Graphics (Singapore) Pte Ltd
Printed and bound in Great Britain by The University Press, Cambridge

British Library Cataloguing in Publication Data
A catalogue record for this book is available from the British Library

Library of Congress Cataloging in Publication Data
A catalogue record for this book has been requested

ISBN 0-415-27028-6

Cover illustration: Masks made by John Crockett for use in the Compass
Players' production of Marlowe's *Dr Faustus* in 1950.

For Marilyn
and in affectionate memory of my father
Thomas 'Ernie' Billingham
and of my father-in-law
Douglas Lee

CONTENTS

INTRODUCTION TO THE SERIES

Contemporary Theatre Studies is a book series of special interest to everyone involved in theatre. It consists of monographs on influential figures, studies of movements and ideas in theatre, as well as primary material consisting of theatre-related documents, performing editions of plays in English, and English translations of plays from various vital theatre traditions worldwide.

Franc Chamberlain

ACKNOWLEDGEMENTS

I would like to thank the following people, without whose help and support this book could not have been completed. In Appendix A, at the back of the book, there is a full list of all former members of the companies who have contributed to making the book possible. The book has its origins in the doctoral thesis I submitted for examination at the University of Leeds in 1994. In that context I wish to thank the All Saints Educational Trust and the Give Peace a Chance Charitable Trust for their invaluable financial support of my research during that period. I would also like to thank Martin Banham, my supervisor, for his constant support of my research project and sense of humour at moments of stress. May I likewise take this opportunity to thank Judy Bottrill and Margaret Smith for their hard work and help in typing revisions and amendments during that time.

In terms of the development of my thesis into this book, I must express my sincere appreciation to my former employers, Bretton Hall College, Wakefield, for offering me a Research Sabbatical in which to write the book. For that invaluable support I wish to thank Paul Cowen, Head of the School of Dance and Theatre, and Tony Green, Deputy Head (Research). In addition I want to acknowledge the help and support offered by other colleagues in that School, especially Linda Taylor, Douglas Hankin, Wendy Johnston, and Arthur Pritchard. In terms of the production and preparation of the book for publication, I would like to express my sincere thanks to Dr Franc Chamberlain who both commissioned it and provided insightful advice through various drafts. I also wish to thank Sally Ashworth for her invaluable hard work and contribution to the final proof-reading and indexing.

I want to thank John Dodds for permission to use his excellent and evocative photographs. In addition, I want to thank Sean Dooley, editor of the *Stoke Evening Sentinel*, for permission to use the backstage photograph of the Century Theatre production of *Othello*. Grateful thanks to Carl Harrison, Chief Curator of the Record Office for Leicestershire, Leicester and Rutland, and Steph Mastoris, Curator at the Snibston Discovery Park, for their advice, help and permission in using and reproducing photographs of Century productions. My thanks also to Cathy Haill, archivist at the Theatre Museum, London, for her advice, help and permission to use and reproduce the Compass Players photographs.

I would like to thank the following friends who have given tireless support and belief in both research and book over the long gestation: Susan Painter, Velda Harris, Frances Dann, Nigel Stewart, Lynn Bains, Bill McDonnell and Maureen Barry.

The book would not have been possible without the help, advice and warm friendship of Wilfred Harrison and Cecil Davies.

Last, but most certainly not least, I must express my debt of thanks and appreciation to Marilyn for her understanding and support, without which I could not have completed this book. Finally, fond thanks to Eve and Chris, Thomas, Sally and Leo, Ruth and William, and my wider family, especially Mum, for their interest, patience and good humour during completion of the book.

LIST OF PLATES

1

INTRODUCTION

The starting point for this book came as a direct consequence of areas of British theatre history and practice that were of interest to me, and also a fortuitous discovery of certain theatre practitioners and companies who had hitherto been unknown, both to myself and also to wider academic research. The discovery occurred by chance during the successful completion of my MA Theatre Studies at the University of Leeds in 1985. As a playwright as well as a researcher, I had long been interested in examining the relationship between a playwright's belief system with the form, structure and content of their work. Consequently, this concern became the focus of my research dissertation and, to this end, I looked to examine a writer whose work had received significant professional production, but who had not received previous academic analysis. On this basis, I selected three plays by the actor, writer and director, Wilfred Harrison whom I had met some twelve months previously. In the midst of one of our regular, recorded interviews related to his work, he mentioned the name of R H Ward and The Adelphi Players. Harrison had begun his professional acting career with this company after seeing them on tour in his native Sheffield some forty years previously. Whilst twentieth-century – and especially post-war – British theatre had always represented one of my principal teaching areas, I had never encountered either Richard Ward or The Adelphis and was intrigued to try and find out more. Further conversations with Wilfred Harrison led to my discovering the existence of John Crockett's Compass Players and Elliott Martin Browne's Pilgrim Players, all of whom had toured theatre to communities and venues between 1940 and the early nineteen fifties.

The final piece in this emerging and fascinating jig-saw was Harrison telling me of the early years and origins of the Century Theatre, a unique touring theatre company in which the auditorium itself, along with the cast and scenery, toured small towns and villages, beginning in 1952.

Whilst I had come across the name of Martin Browne and the Pilgrim Players in guides such as Phyllis Hartnoll's *The Concise Oxford Guide to the Theatre*, and also knew of his connections with Eliot's plays, the other companies and persons were entirely new to me. Not only was I intrigued by these hitherto unknown examples of touring repertory theatre, but I was also increasingly certain that they represented an unjustly unrecognised aspect of relatively recent British social, cultural and theatrical history. When I then read a copy of Ward's manifesto article 'Theatre of Persons', published in *The Adelphi Magazine* [1941] and discovered his commitment to a radical overhaul of theatre practice, and also to a wider ideological climate of political and cultural change, my interest was confirmed. Amongst other things, Ward had been a conscientious objector during the Second World War, as well as an active member of the Independent Labour Party and the Peace Pledge Union.[1] His ideological basis for his proposed 'Theatre of Persons' was driven by a passionate commitment to a revival of the dynamic relationship between art and ethics, resulting in a vibrant theatre that was broadly humanistic, whilst retaining a Hegelian, quasi-religious dimension. With Harrison and Crockett sharing broadly similar philosophical ground with Ward, and Martin Browne motivated by the potential he saw within the revival of religious drama, there seemed to be a very real sense in which a study of these four theatre companies might justifiably be called 'Theatres of Conscience'.

At the time, when I first came across these companies, I was also, by synchronicity, committed to re-examining my own personal interest in left-field politics and a non-orthodox, neo-Quaker [2] ethical perspective. This dialectical process of ideological debate has continued in the ensuing period, and I would want to acknowledge the extent to which the research for my book has helped to challenge and stimulate that debate for me. Whilst I had naturally been aware of well-documented initiatives such as Joan Littlewood's Theatre Workshop and also the Unity Theatre, my discovery of companies such as The Adelphis and Compass who were contemporaneous to them excited and engaged me enormously.

My methodological approach has entailed the close reading and analysis of substantial amounts of unique primary source material as well as consulting an increasingly wide range of secondary sources. I have been most fortunate indeed to have access to a wide range of primary material, previously unexamined, especially in relation to the Adelphi Players and the Century Theatre. For most of this material, I am particularly indebted to Cecil Davies and Wilfred Harrison. Both were former Adelphi members at different stages and Harrison, after also acting occasionally with the Compass Players, went on to co-found the Century Theatre with Richard Ward and the engineer/designer, John Ridley. I am also most grateful to all other surviving company members across the four companies whom I have been

1.   Peace Pledge Union. This organisation is discussed in some detail later in this chapter. Founded by Canon Dick Shepherd in 1936, the PPU represented a broad affiliation of pacifist and anti-militarist viewpoints.
2.   Quakers. The Society of Friends, more commonly known as the Quakers, is discussed in some detail later in this chapter and also in the context of chapter three, in relation to Ward's ideological position. Originating as a radical, non-conformist, Christian sect at the time of the English Civil War, the Quakers continue to be active on a global basis in our contemporary world. Whilst Christian in origin, Quakers are pluralistic in practice and emphasise both the individual spiritual journey and also the collective opposition to all forms of discrimination and oppression. Whilst not a Quaker myself, I attend Quaker meetings – characterized by shared and silent contemplation – on a regular basis.

able to contact, and all of whom have been most generous and supportive in both time and the loan of primary source materials and other documentary evidence. A special thanks in this respect should also go to Pamela Dellar for her help on the Compass chapter. A full list of everyone concerned is given in Appendix A at the end of this book.

Finally, may I take this opportunity to thank the archivists at both the London Theatre Museum and the headquarters of The Society of Friends (Quakers), and particularly William Hetherington, archivist at the Peace Pledge Union, for their invaluable help in making available both masks and designs by John Crockett and, at the PPU, various primary and secondary sources relating to the Peace Pledge Union and Richard Ward.

Researching a previously disregarded area of relatively recent British theatre history has its obvious rewards but also inherent difficulties. To begin with, whilst I had access to the kind of extensive primary source material referred to above such as photographs, newspaper reviews, sketches, programmes etc, there was generally a shortage of direct secondary source material from which to measure my own analysis and conclusions. There is no reference at all in any of my secondary reading to The Adelphi Players, whilst the Compass Players were effectively unrecognised with the exception of a brief reference in Christine Redington's *Can Theatre Teach?* There is substantial, though largely anecdotal, material in Pamela Dellar's edited collection of personal reminiscences of the Compass: *Plays Without Theatres*. Also, George Ineson's autobiographical, and necessarily subjective *Community Journey* provides a valuable insight into aspects of nineteen-thirties' and forties' leftist concerns, namely psychoanalysis and experiments with community living. As far as the Pilgrim Players are concerned they represent a double difficulty. Firstly, they offer the least available primary source material available of the four companies under discussion Secondly, the three principal secondary source texts which relate to them are entirely autobiographical [*Pilgrim Story* and *Two In One*] or, in the case of *The Making of T S Eliot's Plays*, reflect the personal memories and subjective evaluation of Martin Browne.

Largely as a result of Martin Browne's wider reputation as a theatre director, particularly in relation to Eliot's plays, there are other occasional references to the Pilgrims in George Rowell and Anthony Jackson's excellent study of the development of British regional theatre *The Repertory Movement* and also in Norman Marshall's personal account of non-commercial theatre between the wars *The Other Theatre*. Finally, as regards the Century Theatre, other than Alan Hankinson's creditable account of the company's history *The Blue Box*, I have been unable to discover any other published critical analysis of that unique touring theatre. Consideration of the analysis of first and secondary source material, and the criteria by which one evaluates and assesses their comparative value as evidence, is clearly an essential and fundamental basis for any academic research. This naturally involves the careful cross-checking of references and sources. Therefore, such considerations were clearly in my mind when I first began my research for this book. For example, in the study of various newspaper critical reviews of The Adelphi Players in performance, I recognised that the significance and value of these reviews as evidence upon which to base an objective assessment of their performance style and standard must attempt to be subject to wider criteria. This was especially so because of the nature of most of the Adelphi's earlier, touring work. During that period, from 1941 until 1946, they were performing under wartime conditions and in non-theatre venues. They were reviewed principally by smaller regional newspapers under circumstances in which it was unlikely that the reviewers would necessarily be specialist theatre critics. One has to be cautious, therefore, in accrediting an informed and reliable significance to all of their evaluations of the Company in performance.

Similarly, the many personal reminiscences that were made available to me through interviews or correspondence, whilst invaluable as first-hand, eye-witness accounts of life with the companies, must naturally be subjected to the critical scrutiny of both their subjectivity and the selectivity of memory, especially over a period of forty or fifty years in most cases. This said, I have tried to carefully balance and objectively assess such primary source materials through cross-referencing and, where possible, through using the relatively objective distance afforded through secondary critical sources, where they have existed. Perhaps the most significant issue that arises from these methodological considerations is that of the difficulty of reconstruction when the nature of the evidence is of the kind that I have identified. This is not an issue that one can, or should, attempt to deal with in any sense of seeking to define ready conclusions or resolutions. To summarise for the purposes of this introduction, my methodological guidelines and principles have been, firstly, to read closely all visually primary source material as evidence of the working practices and performances of the four companies. Secondly, I have sought to evaluate carefully all other documentary, primary source material in the form of written recollections, personal memories expressed orally in interview and recorded, or written minutes of company meetings etc and to try to balance the insight and evidence that such material offers with its essentially inherent subjectivity. Thirdly, and finally, I have sought, as a matter of course, to substantiate such evidence, where possible, with secondary source material. In summarising my methodological approach in this way, and having regard for what lessons might be learned from my enterprise by future workers of theatre history, I also wish to establish clearly the inevitable limits that one must work within in this kind of study.

Owing to the travelling character of the four companies concerned and the social and cultural conditions of wartime Britain in which two of them functioned, they were inevitably performing in constantly changing, non-standard venues to similarly transient and diverse audiences. Social and cultural activities are necessarily suspended and altered under such conditions. This factor inevitably effects the formal recording and critical reporting of cultural activities such as theatre-going. Therefore the transient nature of the companies under discussion and the dislocated, altered social and cultural context in which they functioned all limit the kind of research material that would give evidence of audience composition and response to the work and its wider critical reception. Throughout my researching and writing of this book I have sought to consider and examine the nature of the relationship between the ideological and philosophical basis for the companies' work and their structure, artistic policy and repertory. Furthermore, I have been mindful to try and place their work and achievements in the wider context of touring professional, largely non-commercial repertory theatre to previously theatreless communities in non-standard venues. In addition, and crucially, I have also sought to define and evaluate the work and ethos of the companies in terms of the wider social, cultural and political conditions of British society both pre-1939 and post-1945. It became my growing conviction, as research and writing developed, that here were four small companies who represented small, but significant, links in both the narrative of twentieth-century British theatre and aspects of its defining character. Within the mosaic of companies and individuals such as Joan Littlewood's Theatre Workshop, Norman Marshall and The Gate and other exponents of left-field and progressive theatre, The Adelphis, Pilgrims, Compass and Century require and deserve appropriate recognition and evaluation.

Theatres of Conscience – the social, cultural and political background of the nineteen thirties

In this concluding section of my introduction, I intend to look at some of the key areas of British social, cultural and political life in the decade leading up to the outbreak of war in 1939. Both Richard Ward and Elliot Martin Browne in particular were engaged in issues relating to the questioning, nature and – in Browne's case especially – the affirmation of religious belief. For both men, there was also a clear question to be addressed of the relationship between belief, ethics and theatre as an art form. Whilst Browne would throughout his life subscribe to a deeply-felt Anglo-Catholicism, Ward's activities and energies led him into areas of more radical analysis. Along with his friend, John Crockett, who in the nineteen thirties was a member of the Communist Party of Great Britain, Ward's activities and writing for the Peace Pledge Union signal some of the principal ethical and ideological considerations of the broadly left Popular Front of the nineteen thirties. The following extract from a letter by Ward to Crockett in 1941 strongly conveys their passionate reaction against the existing political and cultural establishment:

> There is that much comfort in the war – that the bomb-dropping is nothing more than the shitting-process of a decrepit and incontinent organism mortally scared.

> Why don't more people of our generation understand what they're fighting for
> at the behest of the State, the Established Church and the Devil himself? (a fine
> unholy trinity) [3]

Many artists, writers and intelligentsia on the broad left would have
subscribed to similar sentiments. As Angus Calder astutely observed in his
classic socio-historical study *The People's War*:

> In Establishment circles the Church of England was always seen as a useful channel
> of nationalist propaganda – 'the Tory Party at Prayer' … But its loyal jingoism in
> the First World War had served only to discredit it with many thinking people,
> especially of the younger generation. [4]

There was the rapidly growing realisation throughout the thirties that art
was inescapably bound up with ethics. Associated with this was the
conviction that there was an inseparable relationship between the public and
the private self. This theme could be seen quite transparently – though not
necessarily successfully – in Auden and Isherwood's political verse drama
The Ascent of F6, in which the hero, Ransom, is as much engaged in an Oedipal
struggle with the omnipresence of his mother, as in resisting the attempts by
a Fascist state to exploit his attempted conquest of the mountain, F6. Auden
and Isherwood's involvement with Communism in this period and Ward's
passing involvement with the ILP offer helpful reference points for an
understanding of the 'Pink Thirties' as Ronald Blythe refers to the decade in
his collection of essays about the period, *The Age of Illusion*. In terms of the
incongruous confluence between religious belief and Marxist conviction, it
was the emergence of verse drama as possibly the principal experimental
dramatic genre in this period that made such a paradox possible. Christopher
Innes expresses this point most effectively:

> In more general terms [the] combination of revolutionary politics with religious
> fervour became the key note for non-naturalistic drama of the period ... As Eliot
> remarked in 1934: 'Only a cause can give the bond, the common assumptions
> between author and audience which the serious dramatist needs. There are only
> two causes now of sufficient seriousness, and they are mutually exclusive: the
> Church and Communism.' [5]

Eliot himself had experimented with a more overtly expressionistic style,
carried from Europe by the influence of Brecht, in his early verse drama
Sweeney Agonistes (1928).

---

3.   Ward in letter to John Crockett, dated '28 February 1941, by kind permission of Wilfred
Harrison, joint Literary Executor of Richard Ward's estate.
4.   Angus Calder, *The People's War – Britain 1939–1945*, (Jonathan Cape, 1969), p.48l.
5.   Christopher Innes, *Modern British Drama 1890–1990*, (Cambridge University Press, 1992),
p.378.

Indeed, this production with its innovative use of dance and masks, was presented by Rupert Doone's The Group Theatre in 1934 and then in a double-bill with Auden's early morality play, *The Dance of Death*, in 1935. Doone's company are more usually known for their collaboration with Auden, Isherwood and Britten, who composed much of the music for their productions. Such diversity of ideological motivation and commonality of form and genre characterises much of the theatrical experimentation of the period. Therefore, in the same year that The Group Theatre were presenting Eliot's expressionistic experiment, Martin Browne was directing Eliot's religious verse drama *The Rock* at Sadler's Wells. As the first ever, newly appointed Religious Drama Advisor, Browne was to be a leading figure in the re-emergence of religious verse drama, a genre explored by Richard Ward in his play *Holy Family* (1941). Rupert Doone was a charismatic and talented dancer, if a difficult person, who had worked with Diaghilev and who, in conjunction with artists such as those already mentioned plus Tyrone Guthrie, was now exploring a movement-based, non-naturalistic approach to theatre. In his use of dance, masks, music and mime, there are clear parallels between Doone's work and the experimental style of John Crockett. Throughout the nineteen thirties there was a rich interplay of artistic experimentation across film making – through John Grierson, Paul Rotha and the GPO Film Unit – literature and theatre. Most of this cultural activity was characterised by the broad ethical and political awareness already identified, whether it contextualised itself in a formally Marxist, broadly leftist, or even in Christian religious terms. It is precisely this diverse context of cultural initiatives and production which, I believe, must be understood in order to fully understand and foreground the emergence and work of the Adelphis, Pilgrims and Compass.

In relation to the Century Theatre, I will argue that its origins, achievements and, ultimately, its difficulties, arose from a fusion of those pre-war values in a rapidly changing, post-war environment. None of the first three companies were 'political' companies in any common sense of that term and in fact Ward had reached a position where he was opposed to agit-prop, propagandist theatre. In 1942, he was quoted as saying that 'The Unity Theatre has died of propaganda', perhaps echoing Auden's concerns – from a speech delivered in 1938 [6] – with a reductive kind of political drama in which characters became two-dimensional stereotypes such as "Striving" or "Rabble". Returning to the three companies, whilst they were neither political theatre companies nor even 'pacifist' or 'religious' companies, it is my contention that, in their broader ideological and aesthetic concerns, they did embody significant preoccupations and initiatives from that pre-war period. In this respect, I believe that they were part and parcel of a broader movement within the non-commercial theatre of that time towards a more progressive, artistically accountable and democratic theatre. This movement, discussed

---

6.   W H Auden, 'The Future of English Poetic Drama', 1938.

so cogently in Rowell and Jackson's *The Repertory Movement*, had its roots in the reforms sought by Shaw, Granville-Barker and Archer at the turn of the century. It is this movement and the more specific constituent initiatives of the nineteen thirties that I now intend to address.

> Already at the turn of the century, the idea of repertory as a form of theatre opposed in every way to the dominant commercial theatre of the time – had become an integral part of the developing concern with the future of the theatre in Britain. It had become inseparably linked to such other central issues as the need to establish a state-subsidised national theatre organised on repertory principles, the need to encourage new British playwrights, and the need to raise the general standards of production At the same time, awareness was growing of the theatre's potency as an educative as well as an artistic medium, and therefore of its importance in the cultural life of the country as a whole. [7]

In a sense many of these concerns identified by Rowell and Jackson in the emerging repertory movement were central to much of the thinking and activities of Martin Browne, Richard Ward, John Crockett and Wilfred Harrison. In the later stages of chapter three, I include reference to the Adelphis engaging in the debate concerning any future National Theatre, one moreover which would recognise the value, importance and involvement of theatre outside of London, rather than the creation of a monolithic, metropolitan-based institution. Furthermore the commitment to improving standards of production and an over-riding sense of the educative and cultural function of theatre, in addition to its role as entertainment, was always present throughout all four companies. I shall now summarise some of the significant non-commercial theatrical initiatives of the nineteen thirties, including the specifically politically motivated companies such as those involved in the Workers' Theatre Movement and the Unity Theatre, which grew out of those smaller, amateur workers' groups. Such companies, as Sidnell states in the following quotation from his *Dances of Death – The Group Theatre of London of the Thirties*, could not be separated entirely from the wider social and political unease of the period:

> The theatre was in a condition of continuous and intensifying revolution for virtually the whole period from about 1890 to 1939 during which it was subject to fundamental economic and technological changes and was beset by wave on wave of would-be reformers intent on restoring its grasp on reality, its communal role, and its vitality as a literary medium and as confluence of the arts. [8]

---

7.   George Rowell and Anthony Jackson, *The Repertory Movement: A History of Regional Theatre in Britain*, (Cambridge University Press, 1984), p.2.
8.   Michael Sidnell, *Dances of Death: The Group Theatre of London in the Thirties*, (London, Faber, 1984), p.25.

The clamour for artistic and structural reform within British theatre came against the continuing backdrop of a sterile commercial theatre that seemed deliberately immune to both its detractors within the wider profession, and also the political and social turmoil of the nineteen thirties. Ward wrote of this theatrical establishment as 'a garish and showy facade, reared upon the shifting sands of fashion', whilst Ronald Blythe observes that:

> Shaftesbury Avenue was glossy as a chestnut through the smooth ministrations of Frederick Lonsdale, Noel Coward and their debtors. The audiences were captive and knew what they liked, and the dramatists dished it out to them, season after season ... The mechanics of the play were compressed into three acts of mellifluous middle-class conversation. [9]

Amongst those who sought to challenge this complacent theatrical orthodoxy were those such as Terence Gray at the Cambridge Festival Theatre, J B Fagan at the Oxford Playhouse, Peter Godfrey and later Norman Marshall at The Gate, London, Barry Jackson and the Birmingham Rep and perhaps most well known of all, Lilian Baylis at the Old Vic. In addition, as well as Doone's already mentioned Group Theatre, there was Ashley Dukes' Mercury Theatre which played such an important role in the revival of verse drama, and of which more will be discussed in the following chapter. It is essential as well to recognise the important role that the Workers' Theatre Movement played in helping to define the political climate of theatrical innovation in this period.

The Workers' Theatre Movement (1926–35) was founded to 'conduct working-class propaganda and agitation through dramatic representation'. Agit-prop theatre originated in the aftermath of the Russian Revolution as a substitute for newsprint, to spread information and the party-line through a widely dispersed and largely illiterate population; and the typical form of short sketches illustrating political commentary was developed by the 'Blue Shirts' troupe, an off-shoot of the Russian Institute of Journalism. [10]

The WTM was a loose confederation of various small amateur theatre groups, its members almost exclusively from the working-class. One of the principal activists, and possibly the movement's most significant writer, was Tom Thomas. Amongst his most recognised achievements was a dramatisation of Walter Greenwood's novel of poverty, deprivation and resistance *Love on The Dole*. Activists such as Thomas had visited the Soviet Union and witnessed the use of drama in that revolutionary climate. Through these contacts, the influence of Brecht and Piscator filtered through and became important means for other activists such as Joan Littlewood and Ewan McColl to develop their performance style through their Theatre of Action (1932–4). Theatre of Action had itself evolved from McColl's earlier group,

---

9.   Ronald Blythe, *The Age of Illusion: some glimpses of Britain between the Wars 1919–40*, (Oxford University Press, 1983), p.116.
10. Innes, p.72.

Red Megaphones, and itself became the basis for Theatre Workshop. During the War, Theatre Workshop and The Adelphi Players were to quite often follow similar touring routes and there was certainly one occasion when Littlewood's company and the Compass had both, independently, received board and lodging at Ormesby Hall in the north of England. Internal disputes and the failure of the Central Committee of the Communist Party of Great Britain to value and support the work of the WTM led to its decline and eventual re-formation into the Unity Theatre. Whilst there is not the opportunity or necessity to enter into any deeper analysis for the demise of the WTM, it is perhaps worth quoting again from Innes who asserts that:

> As with the gap between political forecast and historical actuality in a script like 'John Bullion', the simplified analysis of the Agitprop mode turns its dramatic statement into wish-fulfilment. Even in the widespread unemployment of the thirties, it had little demonstrable political effect. [11]

Whilst I do not want to stretch inappropriate connections between such a diverse range of theatres from The Gate through to the Red Megaphones, there was, amongst those non-commercial companies amongst which the Unity would eventually be included, a commitment to perform plays in repertoire that were of artistic value, but which would not find a platform within the hegemony of commercial theatre. These plays chosen in repertoire across the various companies represented a catholicity that in itself reflected the tastes of the individual producers and entrepreneurs. Nevertheless, one can state with some certainty that an underlying rationale in the selection of plays in companies from the Cambridge Festival Theatre through to The Adelphi Players, was the simple notion of 'good plays'. Such plays would have a transparent quality, clear artistic merit and often an accompanying ethical or political dimension to them. I am, of course, fully aware that this notion of 'good plays' is open to the clear criticism of class-based, elitist notions of what constitutes 'good art'. Companies such as The Adelphi Players were sometimes subject to the charge of patronizing their audiences, as the following reviewer from the *Doncaster Gazette* made clear in 1943:

> … The Adelphi Players … have an unfortunate penchant for putting on plays in the spirit of giving the public what The Adelphi Players think is good for them, whether the public like it or not. One does not blame the average family of home-holiday makers from avoiding *The Duchess of Malfi*, an Elizabethan tragedy that might possibly interest the keen student of drama but would certainly pass over the heads of ordinary people. [12]

Nevertheless, all four companies under examination maintained a

---

11. Ibid, p.74.
12. *Doncaster Gazette*, 12 August 1943.

fundamental commitment to select plays for repertory which they felt were worth producing because of what they had to say and the theatrical language through which that was expressed.

In the programme/prospectus for The Adelphi Players circulated in 1943, this sentiment was expressed more formally:

> It is becoming increasingly evident that the people of Britain feel the need and the value of their cultural heritage in the darkness of the present. Where the theatre is concerned, there is clear and growing demand, not only for plays which will provide entertainment ... but more especially for plays which are essentially re-creative in the sense of building up the human mind and spirit. The Adelphi Players believe that the collapse of the familiar social order of the past decade is bringing a new and more abundant life in the theatre. [13]

This important sense in which the conditions of war facilitated a renewed interest in cultural activities is central, I believe, to a further understanding of why companies such as the Pilgrims and Compass were both necessary and, basically, welcomed. There is a very important sense in which the companies were very much products of specific historical circumstances and, simultaneously, embodied and signalled them. A T Tolley identifies this phenomenon of wartime conditions in his insightful evaluation *The Poetry of the Forties*:

> During the war there was a remarkable interest in nearly all cultural activities. People were thrown back upon themselves because the black-out and other features of the war inhibited social gatherings. Many of those in the forces or civil defence found themselves with a great deal of time on their hands far from any source of entertainment other than a book or the radio. Above all, in the face of the complete disruption of their lives and the possibility of sudden death, people began to think about fundamental things and to seek what would sustain them emotionally. [14]

Whilst the conditions of wartime undoubtedly highlighted that sense of the value of 'cultural heritage in the darkness of the present' and whilst such sentiments were open to the exploitation of government propaganda, the companies were nevertheless building upon the earlier precedent of the value of theatre asserted by those such as Bayliss and Marshall. To the extent that they were taking an 'alternative repertoire' to communities, audiences and venues that had previously remained theatreless, their efforts and achievements warrant proper recognition.

Returning to the wider cultural context, one of the enduring and potent icons of the thirties is that of the politically-motivated and committed poet.

---

13. The Adelphi Players, Programme and Prospectus, 1943.
14. A T Tolley, *The Poetry of the Forties*, (Manchester University Press, 1985), p.3.

As Blythe observes:

> It was the poets and not the politicians who were the first to sense a new climate of violence as reactionary elements the world over, but particularly in Germany, saluted each other and fascism emerged. [15]

The poets that he implicitly refers to – Auden, Spender, MacNeice and Day Lewis amongst others – were all very much of a certain class with all of its accompanying status and privilege: the English upper-middle class. Ward and Crockett shared a similar, public school background. Another younger poet of this class and generation, John Cornford, was the founder of the radical student organisation, the Federation of Socialist Societies, at Cambridge. He also became the first Englishman to volunteer to fight in the Spanish Civil War, dying in action in 1936. The Spanish Civil War, with its complex web of idealism, realpolitik and betrayals, was memorably evoked through Orwell's *Homage to Catalonia*. In his account, he presented a harrowing and darkly depressing vision of indiscriminate suffering inflicted by the cynical political opportunism of both the fascist and Stalinist forces.

The tragic and wretched conclusion to the Spanish Civil War offered a terrible prescience of 1939 and confirmed the growing sense of moral impotence and confusion felt by many on the left:

> The hope of intellectual radicals like Spender that the anti-fascist political movements of the thirties could prevent a second world war was shattered: they felt that they had been betrayed into war by the cowardice and stupidity of a conservative establishment. [16]

One of the significant contributors to the creation of a broad left Popular Front in the nineteen thirties was Victor Gollancz. Through his publishing house and his formation of The Left Book Club with its accompanying magazine *Left News*, Gollancz and his enterprise created the opportunity for a broad range of leftist literature to be published, distributed and read. Furthermore, his project also helped to build up a network of discussion groups around the country who engaged in debate about social and political issues of the day. By the end of 1936 from between 150 and 200 Left Book Club circles had sprung up all over the country. Articles in *Left News* began to draw people's attention to the way civil liberties were being threatened, particularly in the Mosleyite persecution of the Jews in the East End. [17]

In addition to *Left News*, there were many other literary journals in circulation at this time. These included *New Atlantis*, Claud Cockburn's *The Week*, Middleton Murry's *The Adelphi* – from which Ward took inspiration in

---

15. Blythe, p.106.
16. Tolley, p.3.
17. Blythe, p.116.

naming his company – and *Left Review*. In the same period the Communist Party of Great Britain, which in 1930 had 1,376 members, had passed 15,500 members by the close of the thirties. All of this political activism and consciousness-raising was occuring irrevocably in the context of a society and world in which the capitalist economy was facing crisis.

This political scenario simultaneously created the circumstances of which the emergence of fascism in Europe was arguably both a consequence, symptom and even, I would assert, a rationale. In the process, the underlying economic system survived under the guise of an arguably nominal social and political democracy. America had 12 million unemployed in 1933, whilst, in that same year, Germany and Britain followed with respective figures of 4.6 million, and 2.85 million, unemployed. At the same time there were incidents in which a number of the unemployed lay down as a protest demonstration in the foyer of the Savoy Hotel. Meanwhile, at Oxford, Dick Shepherd was establishing the Peace Pledge Union, an increasingly active and eloquent platform for the expression of broadly leftist, anti-militaristic and pacifist thinking.

The Reverend Dick Shepherd was vicar of St Martin-in-the-Fields and Dean of Canterbury and had formerly been an Army Chaplain. Shepherd had been appalled by the suffering he had witnessed in this role during the First World War. Thereafter he became convinced that the spirit of the Christian teaching of love for one's neighbour, and the common humanity of all people, was incompatible with the institutionalised violence of war. Whilst his initiative represented an act of personal ethical conviction, it should also be viewed as in the context of the origins of pacifism and its renewed growth in this century. Furthermore, in terms of the importance of religious belief to both Elliot Browne and Ward, albeit expressed in different ways, it is also essential to provide some of the wider context regarding the relationship of church to society in the pre-war period.

> Mass Observation, in a survey at the end of the war, found that about two-thirds of men and four-fifths of women, in a London suburb, said they believed in God, and only about one person in twenty was ready to profess atheism. But six out of ten said they never went to church. [18]

Certainly, decline in church attendance had its roots well established in the previous century with a particularly significant failure to by the church to engage in the collective lives of working-class people. In terms of the early decades of the twentieth century, there was a crisis in the number of ordained ministers needed to sustain parishes, particularly in the larger industrial cities. One example cited by Calder was Birmingham where, in 1938, there had been 178 curates, whilst in 1948, there were only 38. However, despite the prevailing sense of a class-and tradition-bound institution critically out of

---

18. Calder, p.478.

touch with the lives and demands of ordinary people, there was evidence of movements within the broader church throughout the nineteen twenties, thirties and, indeed, into the war years themselves. Shepherd's initiative clearly represents one of these but there were others, including William Temple, George Bell and Cardinal Hinley who was the Catholic Archbishop of Westminster. Hinley had founded 'The Sword of the Spirit', a kind of Catholic-based Popular Front which he hoped would, within an ecumenical and secular partnership, address some of the principal causes of social neglect and injustice. However, the Catholic hierarchy resisted and the project ended with Hinley's death in 1943. Bishop George Bell's contribution to the development of religious verse drama is discussed in more detail in the following chapter. That in itself constituted a significant example of the Church seeking to transcend its own cultural parochialism. However Bell sought to contribute to other progressive, liberal initiatives which deserve recognition.

Bell was an outspoken opponent of the night bombing of German civilian populations and pursued his criticism of government policy, to the point where, in 1943, he was even denied the opportunity to speak at the Battle of Britain Commemoration Service at his own diocesan cathedral at Chichester. Finally, in 1944, he had asked, in the House of Lords, for a formal government statement of policy on the bombing of civilian and non-military populations. Unlike Shepherd, Bell did not hold to a pacifist position but struggled to reconcile his profound indictment of war, with his felt acknowledgement that it represented the only means of defeating the evils of Fascism. Whilst Bell remained alone within the senior Anglican hierarchy in opposing the indiscriminate bombing of German cities, there were other relatively radical voices at work in terms of both analysis and action on social, economic and political issues. William Temple was a prime mover in these initiatives. Just before Christmas in 1940, at which time he was Archbishop of York, he was a cosignatory of an open letter in *The Times* in which five standards were proposed for the more just reordering of society. The most radical proposals concerned the abolition of the extreme inequalities in wealth and possessions and advocated equal educational opportunities for all. Earlier in the following year, 1941, a conference of laity and clergy was called at Malvern under Temple's chairmanship. Significantly in terms of my study, both Middleton Murry – supporter of Ward and The Adelphi Players – and Eliot, personal friend to Martin Browne – were major speakers. The central aim of the conference was to address ways in which the church might contribute to the reconstruction of a more just society in the post-war period. Under Temple's guiding influence, the conference produced two pamphlets called the 'Malvern Findings' which had a joint circulation of over a million.

However, it is significant that Eliot's inherently conservative Anglo-Catholiciam led to him disassociating himself from what was Malvern's principal, radical, findings. This criticized:

… the maintenance of that part of the structure of society, by which the ultimate ownership of the principal industrial resources of the community can be vested in the hands of private owners. [19]

Despite the inevitable reservations of Churchill, it was Temple who was appointed as Archbishop of Canterbury, replacing the retired – theologically and socially conservative – Cosmo Lang. Temple was immensely popular outside the Conservative establishment and was able to draw upon a great amount of popular working-class support, along with that of avowedly, non-religious, atheist socialists such as George Bernard Shaw. It was Shaw who famously declared that 'an archbishop of Temple's enlightenment was a realised impossibility'. Temple's liberal theological analysis is expressed and preserved within his classic *Christianity and the Social Order* (1942) for which he consulted Keynes for advice on economic matters. Temple died suddenly in 1944 and was to be sadly missed by many. During his relatively short lifetime, he had advocated a powerful social and economic critique from within a predominantly conservative Anglican church establishment. Along with Bell, he represented the liberal-radical voice within the church, defending the right to conscientious objection, whilst grappling with the perception that that war must be fought in order to overthrow Nazism.

Having provided a sense of wider debates and initiatives within the church at the time, I now wish to return to a brief account of Shepherd's attempts to mobilise anti-war ideological sentiments into a credible and potent formation: the Peace Pledge Union.

The concept of Christian pacifism can be traced back to George Fox, the founder of the Society of Friends, more commonly known as the Quakers. This seventeenth-century religious group might best be understood as, along with the Diggers and Levellers, expressions of those radical, non-conformist movements which arose out of the ideological struggle which characterised the English Civil War. Critical of, and opposed to, the concept and function of the priest as an intermediary between people and God, Fox and the Quakers also identified the church establishment as synonymous with a corrupt monarchy and secular establishment. Quakers faced persecution – in some cases resulting in death – for their refusal to make an oath to the King and to take up arms. Their form of worship resisted the authoritarian hierarchy of the church and instead was characterized by an open, democratic meeting in which, out of the shared contemplative silence, any person might share their thoughts and understanding. In the latter years of the nineteenth-century and twentieth-century, pacifism became increasingly to be identified with an ethical socialism within British society. Within such an ideological viewpoint, it was argued that in the context of the common humanity of all peoples, war must be viewed as yet another example of the working-classes being exploited and killed in the economic, imperialist interests of the

---

19. Ibid, p.483.

capitalist ruling-class and industrialists. The Independent Labour Party became particularly associated with this essentially Marxist position and its ethos is well expressed in the following quotation from Kier Hardie in 1913:

> All forms of militarism belong to the past ... Militarism and democracy cannot be blended. The workers of the world have nothing to fight each other about ... They have no country. Patriotism is for them a term of no meaning. [20]

Emerging out of this view came the formation of the No-Conscription Fellowship which was founded by the ILP's leader Fenner Brockway in 1914. This organisation, with an initial membership of some three hundred, had its original headquarters at Brockway's home in Derbyshire. Nevertheless, from 1915 onwards, its membership grew so much that they were obliged to rent London offices. It was also in July 1915 that the issue of Conscription became imminent. A national network of local N-CF branches was formed. The N-CF embraced a diverse range of men who, for differing ethical and political reasons, were not prepared to engage in war. These ranged from those known as 'Absolutists' who would not engage in any form of war-related work, to the many who were prepared to take on non-combatant duties. It was an important and influential pressure group for, whilst it could not prevent conscription at the outbreak of war, it did succeed in ensuring that conscientious objection was recognised as grounds for non-conscription in the Military Service Act of 1916. Whilst formal recognition had thus been made, nevertheless this legislation was often either ignored, or unjustly disregarded, by the tribunals which objectors had to face in order to claim their right to resist conscription. In fact, seventy-three conscientious objectors died as a result of the ill-treatment they had to endure whist in custody for their beliefs. There were also appalling instances of the transference of C.O.s to France in May 1916. In an attempt to force C.O.s into combat, these men were placed amongst serving troops and brutally punished for their refusal to comply. These punishments included 'Crucifixion':

> Each of us was placed with our backs to the framework, consisting of uprights at intervals of four to five yards, and cross-beams at a height of about five feet from the ground. Our ankles were tied together and our arms then tied tightly at the wrists to the cross-beams; and we prepared to remain in this position for the next two hours. [21]

Socially, many men who successfully exempted themselves from military service, were ostracised and abused. Another organization from this period which deserves recognition is the Fellowship of Reconciliation, co-founded

20. Kier Hardie, cited in 'War – We Say No', a Peace Pledge Union pamphlet, (PPU, May 1991).
21. Cited in 'The No-Conscription Fellowship – A Souvenir of its work during the years 1914–1919' (N-CF, 1922), p.42. Kindly loaned by Friend's Central Library, Sheffield.

by a German Lutheran and an English Quaker in 1914. It is interesting to note that the young Wilfred Harrison was the FOR secretary for the Sheffield branch, and a Regional Representative on the PPU council. He joined The Adelphi Players after he had seen them in performance in Sheffield in 1942, volunteering his help whilst arranging their accommodation. Other significant developments in the post-1918 period were the establishing of the War Resisters' International [WRI] in 1923 with its declaration that, 'War is a crime against humanity, I am therefore determined not to support any kind of war and to strive for the removal of all causes of war.'

It was against this background, therefore, that Dick Shepherd's founding of the Peace Pledge Union needs to be understood. Pacifism had begun to reach a wider public audience through the controversial motion, voted by 275 votes to 153, at an Oxford Union Debate in February 1933, that 'This House will in no circumstances fight for its King and Country'. The largely right-wing press covered this issue with fervour and it was followed by the right-wing Tory candidate, campaigning on a militarist platform, being defeated by the socialist candidate advocating pacifist principles at the Fulham East by-election. In October 1934, Shepherd sent a letter to the national press saying: "It seems essential to discover whether or not it be true, as we are told, that the majority of thoughtful men in this country are now convinced that war of every kind or for every cause, is not only a denial of Christianity but a crime against humanity, which is no longer to be permitted by civilised people."

He invited men who had so far been silent, to send him a postcard saying that they supported the resolution to "renounce war, and never again, directly or indirectly, support or sanction another." Within two days, 2,500 men responded, and in the next few months the number grew to over 30,000. [22]

An equally important figure in this movement, and for the broader cause of peace through Christian socialism, was George Lansbury. Lansbury was a radical Labour politician and activist, whose values and policies can be clearly contextualised in terms of the wider socialist/pacifist movement discussed previously. He had stood for Parliament at the turn of the century on an anti-Boer War platform, although he was defeated on that occasion. However, he was eventually successful some ten years later, being elected on a socialist manifesto. Lansbury also identified himself with the Suffragette movement, resigning from his seat to stand, again unsuccessfully, on their ideological platform. He was also the editor of the *Daily Herald*, a socialist newspaper and the only paper to substantially and continuously oppose the First World War. He returned to Parliament in 1923 and was leader of the Labour Party from 1931 to 1935. It was in 1935 that Lansbury, along with other well-known figures such as Edmund Blunden and Siegfried Sassoon, joined Shepherd on

---

22. Shepherd, cited in *Peace is the Way: A Guide to Pacifist Views and Actions*, compiled and edited by Cyril Wright and Tony Augarde, (The Lutterworth Press, 1990), p.157.

the platform at a packed-out meeting at the Albert Hall. By the end of the year, the as yet unnamed movement had 80,000 signatories. On 22 May 1936, the movement was officially named as the Peace Pledge Union with women also being invited to join and support its aims. John Crockett and Richard Ward were early members and, in fact, their life-long friendship began through meeting at PPU headquarters where Ward acted as one of a small number of personal assistants to Shepherd. In July of that year, *Peace News*, which had been started separately in June 1936, became the weekly newspaper of the PPU.

Ward wrote two articles for *Peace News* and they offer both further insight into the ethical and political views which informed his pacifism, as well as revealing some of the issues central to PPU thinking at that time. The two articles were called 'What is Non-Violent Technique?' which was published in October 1938, and 'The Human Factor' which was published in 1939. I want to draw on some selected quotations from both of these articles to discuss both Ward's ideological values and aspects of the broader PPU position. In 'What Is Non-Violent Technique?', Ward attempts to define the causes of war and militarism and then proceeds to discuss the plurality of ways in which pacifists can oppose both. He begins by asserting that:

> Pacifism, moreover, must be an immediate struggle against war ... War is not a disease which breaks out here and there in history, but the symptom of a disease which is the actual condition of the present social order, other symptoms of which, capitalism and imperialism, are as inescapable from it and from one another as war is inseparable from it. It is in effect against this unholy trinity, capitalism, imperialism and war, that the pacifist finds himself struggling. [23]

Ward goes on to advocate that the only opposition to this 'disease', itself an expression of a malignant social and economic order, is through non-violence. For Ward, to engage in violence to overcome violence, is both ethically and politically untenable. He develops his analysis of capitalist society as inherently and profoundly immoral:

> The existing order of society is profoundly immoral: the behaviour of its institutions and of those who own or condone them is based on values such as no system of religion or social ethics can accept ... the "values" of acquisitiveness, aggression, self-regard, hatred, violence, oppression and competition. The history of Europe in the last few weeks provided us with examples of this immorality which stink to high heaven. [24]

In this final reference, Ward is alluding to the issue of the effective 'surrender' of Czechoslovakia to the Germans in September 1938, as part of the Munich

---

23. R H Ward, 'What Is Non-Violent Technique?', *Peace Pamphlets*, 11, (1934–40), p.5.
24. Ward, p.7.

'appeasement' agreement. In the final stages of his article, Ward continues by identifying the ethical and other beliefs which might inform a new, alternative social order. He believed that such values could be deduced from within multi-cultural traditions such as Buddhist, Taoist and Christian, adding that these might also be joined by '... Marxism, socialism and anarchism ...'. Ward then introduces the concept of the 'revolutionary pacifist' with whom he appears to identify:

> The conviction of the revolutionary pacifist is the necessity for the building of another social order: any step that he takes in that direction is a step in politics. But the social order he envisages differs radically from that which exists and whose political expression we know only too well; therefore his political action must also differ radically. [25]

This view of revolutionary political action therefore required a transcendence of conventional political activity. This in itself necessitated an attempt to combine a radical, inward transformation with a consequent political dimension. This would be expressed within a programme of radical non-violent resistance to the existing social and political order. These ideas throw important, complementary, light I believe, upon significant elements in relation to Ward's thinking relating to theatre, expressed most clearly in his manifesto article for *The Adelphi* magazine: 'Theatre of Persons'. This article is discussed in more detail in chapter three in my wider analysis of The Adelphi Players.

However, in its ideological combination of radical sociocultural change within the context of a theatre that he envisages 'illuminating' human experience, one can begin to see the concept of the person and the personal as having not only an ethical but also a political value. Ward pursues this further in his second article 'The Human Factor' published just prior to the outbreak of war in 1939. He states that 'What takes place in the greedy heart of one in London may have its effect on the malnourished body of a child on Tyneside'. He proceeds by asserting that:

> A society has no being of its own; it is a collection of individuals and can behave only as those individuals behave. According to what we are, so will our social and moral order be ... We are told that the causes of war are political or economic: this is not looking far enough. Politics and economics are dependent upon human beings. [26]

The 'Human Factor' of the article's title refers once again to a concept of personhood that is essentially ethical, built upon a pluralistic ideological basis with radical, transforming implications for the individual and therefore,

---

25. Ibid, p.8.
26. R H Ward, 'The Human Factor' *Peace Pamphlets*, 11, (1939–40), p. 8.

according to Ward's position, society as well. The weakness in this analysis, it seems to me, is that in focussing upon abstract concepts of ethical value based on unproven assumptions, the contributory, more fundamental implications of class, economic production and exploitation almost become secondary. Put most simply, seriously and vividly, the phenomenon of the rise of fascism in Nazi Germany could not be adequately explained in terms alone of the combined consequences of several million individual German citizens. Towards the end of this article, Ward refers to Hegelian ethics in the same manner that he also employs in 'Theatre of Persons', asserting that: 'We must give our humanity, the factor in us which Hegel recognised when he said "Be a person and treat others like persons"'.

Finally, in his conclusion to his article, he attempts to define 'The Human Factor' in terms that remind me of Orwell's notion of 'decency' as a primary, common ethic upon which socialist values might progress:

> What is this human factor? Call it what you like: a sense of right and wrong, or morality; a fundamentally religious attitude to life and persons; ordinary decency; conscience. [27]

Within a few months of Ward's article effectively forlornly making a plea for decency in the face of the brutal realpolitik of European fascism, a more widely recognised leftist writer of the thirties, Stephen Spender, wrote: "I am going to keep a journal, because I cannot accept the fact that I feel so shattered that I cannot write at all." [28] These are the opening words of a journal that Spender began on 3 September 1939, the date on which Britain declared war on Germany in response to Hitler's invasion of Poland on 1 September. Ultimately, the attempt to organise a united, Popular Front, could not achieve any tangible consequences in terms of government foreign policy. Ward remained critical also of the failure of the broad left, including the PPU, to engage in sufficient numbers or effectiveness with the working-class:

> It is clear that the pacifist movement will achieve little until it makes contact with the people ... In power and in numbers the working-class is the most important section of the people: the pacifist movement will not make contact with the working-class, or become in any true sense a popular movement, until those responsible for it have the imagination to say something to the working-class in terms which it will not only understand but respond to emotionally. [29]

Throughout 1938 and 1939 when these two articles were written and published, the PPU organised campaigns against air raid precautions, issue of gas masks and the re-introduction of conscription. Of especial interest in

---

27. Ibid, p.15.
28. Tolley, p.3.
29. Ward, p.15.

the context of this book's concerns was the existence of agitprop-style theatre activities. Unfortunately, these activities have not, to my knowledge, been formally examined. Like the Unity Theatre and the earlier Workers' Theatre Movement, this work was almost certainly amateur in status. The titles of two plays that were performed, on a mobile basis, are known. These are *Idiot's Delight* (by the American author, Robert E Sherwood) in 1936 and *The Pacifist's Progress* (author unknown). Just prior to this period of activism, Dick Shepherd had died suddenly in 1937. Nevertheless, by April 1940, membership – which from 1936 had included women – was up to a highest-ever 136,000. Even after the outbreak of war, some PPU activists continued their struggle: In 1940 six leading members of the Union, including Alex Wood, Chairman, and Stuart Morris, General Secretary, were persecuted under the Defence Regulations for endeavouring to cause disaffection among persons in H M Service by publishing a poster with the wording "War will cease when men refuse to fight. What are you going to do about it?" The defendants were bound over for twelve months. [30] In February 1940 a Women's Peace Day was also organised, its publicity leaflets stating that, 'Women have worked for years in the cause of humanity and peace. Now they see that the hope of achievement lies in a united demand that constructive ways should be explored' [Hetherington, *Resisting War*, Peace Pledge Union, 1986]. In terms of the touring work of the Pilgrim Players, The Adelphi Players and The Compass during the war years, it is interesting to note other examples of touring, or mobile, theatre. As I've previously stated, it appears that the PPU were active in this sense, as were the Unity Theatre, who, like the Pilgrims and Adelphis, took mobile theatre units into the tube stations doubling as air raid shelters.

Furthermore, through the transference of Unity personnel such as Ted Willis and Andre van Gysegham into the ABCA Play Unit, the techniques of the documentary Living Newspaper spread to performances to the troops. Living Newspaper was a form of consciousness-raising theatre that had its origins in the Soviet Blue Blouse troupes of the immediate post-Revolutionary period. This method of dramatising contemporary political events and issues was also taken up and used by groups within the WTM and also the Federal Theatre Project groups in America during the Depression:

> As its name suggests, it took up issues of burning political and social interest, bringing them to life through a portrayal of their effects on the life of the average woman or man. The abandonment of traditional plot structure ... was complemented by ... the exploitation of all dramatic resources (music, megaphone, lighting effects, recitation, antiphony, pantomime, dance and dramatic elements) ... the Living Newspaper was based on the idea of 'self-made' theatre. [31]

---

30. William Hetherington, *Resisting War: 50 Years working for Peace*, (Peace Pledge Union Press, 1986), p.6.
31. Gustav Klaus, *The Literature of the Labour: 200 Years of Working-Class Writing*, (The Harvester Press, 1985), pp.169–70.

The ABCA unit was the acronym for the Army Bureau of Current Affairs. Formed later in the war, nevertheless by June 1944 the Play Unit had given fifty eight performances to around twenty thousand soldiers. Like the companies under examination, the ABCA Play Unit also worked on the basis of all company members sharing equal responsibilities in terms of company organisation and production. Due to the nature of the Play Unit's work and involvement of socialist theatre workers such as Willis and others, Churchill tried, unsuccessfully, to put an end to their activities. [Davies, *Other Theatres*, Macmillan, 1987.]

R H Ward, in the minutes of an Adelphi Company Meeting in 1942, reviews the theatre of the period and states that: 'So far as I can see, our day has no theatrical heart; the Old Vic is essentially a survival; the plays of Auden and Isherwood seem to have been abortive; the Unity Theatre has died of propaganda.' It is interesting to note that the two companies and two collaborative writers he selects reflect important reference points in the theatre of this period, with all of its complex social, cultural and political turmoil. When he refers to the Old Vic as being 'essentially a survival' is he referring to perhaps to the difficult period just prior to, and following on from, the death of the company's charismatic founder, Lilian Baylis, in 1937? Although the Vic is often discussed as if it were a homogeneous entity, the theatre had passed though six distinct phases by 1937. When Tyrone Guthrie took over from Baylis following her death, the company had as Norman Marshall believed, 'lost both its audience and was heavily in debt.' Its artistic reputation was partially revived through Guthrie's 1939-40 season with a commitment to casting an 'all-star' company including Robert Donat, John Gielgud, Lewis Casson, Cathleen Nesbitt and Fay Compton amongst others. In November 1940, the Governors took the much criticised decision of taking the company out of London to a regional base, the Victoria Theatre, Burnley. From there, productions were taken on tour to the provinces with the support of CEMA, the forerunner of the Arts Council and an organisation which is discussed in more detail in chapters two and three. In chapter three, John Headley, one of the early Adelphi members, recalls meeting with Sybil Thordike and Lewis Casson when they toured with the Old Vic's *Macbeth* to the mining areas of South Wales.

Undoubtedly, the Old Vic were able to draw upon material resources and highly experienced actors to support their tours during wartime. Nevertheless, there was criticism from many quarters that the company should have stayed in London during the war – where companies such as the Pilgrims and Adelphis continued to perform – and, at the time of Ward's observation, it is arguably true that the Old Vic was living on its past reputation, rather than offering a new initiative and example.

I have already referred to the plays of Auden and Isherwood and The Group Theatre. Alongside the emergence of the Unity Theatre had been the Westminster Theatre, like the Unity, a converted chapel. The Westminster Theatre was, essentially, a venue rather than a specific, producing company.

It was associated with a wide range of non-commercial theatre in the thirties, ranging from The Group productions through to the London Masque Theatre under J B Priestley, before eventually falling into the ownership of the Oxford Moral Rearmament movement. This movement was inherently conservative and reactionary in composition and aims, seeking the solution to the social and economic problems of the day through a re-awakening of traditional moral values. The movement attracted a degree of popular support though mainly from the lower-professional, conservative middle-classes, including the young Mary Whitehouse. In itself, it represents another factor in the wider picture of ideological, religious and ethical debate during the pre-war period. During their use of the Westminster Theatre premises, Auden and Isherwood's plays sought to combine movement, verse and Marxism into a potent theatrical style. Nevertheless, lack of money and internal disputes conspired to undermine the company and its work. Auden and Isherwood failed to build upon the modest success of *The Ascent of F6* and left England for America at the outbreak of war.

There were those on the left, like Orwell, who were contemptuously critical of this decision, seen as a mixture of moral cowardice and the abnegation of the artist's public responsibilities. There is no evidence of Ward's views on this matter, but he may have believed that their artistic experimentation had failed in its intentions and that, furthermore, their departure from England terminated any further contribution to the development of progressive theatre within Britain. However, in terms of the inter-disciplinary use and exploration of verse, dance and music, they had been engaged in a form of theatre that re-appeared in work such as the Compass production of the verse play by the New Zealand poet Charles Brasch: *The Quest*.

Finally, in his reference to the Unity has having 'died of Propaganda', one must assume that Ward was referring to the more politically explicit work of the Living Newspaper style and format. Ward was opposed to the idea and function of drama-as-propaganda, believing that it inevitably resulted in naive and representational kinds of characterisation and dialogue. As Innes observes when discussing Tom Thomas' use of what he called Dialectical Realism, 'the X-Ray picture of society and social forces':

> In practice this led to melodramatic simplifications of social reality, with the devil as a top-hatted financier ... or Hitler as the embodiment of Capitalism. [32]

By 1947, the Unity itself had "left behind the rather narrow propaganda play, apt in its day but no longer adequate for the time ... The people have developed a breadth of interest and confidence which demands a new expression." I shall discuss the wider implications of this change in role for the Unity in my final chapter.

---

32. Innes, pp.72–3.

ALHAMBRA ALEXANDRIA

Tél. 32-26 — Manager: Bettino CONEGLIANO — Tél. 32-26

COMMENCING WEDNESDAY, MARCH 5th 1930

EDWARD STIRLING AND THE CELEBRATED

THE ENGLISH PLAYERS

Directors: EDWARD STIRLING and Frank Reynolds

In a Repertory of Plays

Friday March 7th. at 9.15 p.m.	"WHITE CARGO" by LEON GORDON (From the Playhouse Theatre London)
Saturday March 8th at 9.15 p.m.	JOURNEY'S END (LE GRAND VOYAGE) by R. C. SHERRIFF
Sunday March 9th at 9.15 p.m.	"THE IMPORTANCE OF BEING EARNEST" by OSCAR WILDE
Monday March 10th at 9.15 p.m.	"THE FIRST Mrs. FRASER" by St JOHN ERVINE (Now being played at the Haymarket Theatre London)
Tuesday March 11th at 9.15 p.m.	"JUNO AND THE PAYCOCK" by SEAN O'CASEY
Wednesday March 12th at 9.15 p.m.	"THIS WAS A MAN" by NOEL COWARD
Thursday March 13th. at 9.15. p.m.	JOURNEY'S END (LE GRAND VOYAGE) by R. C SHERRIFF (as played by this company over 250 times)
Friday March 14th. at 9.15 p.m.	"ESCAPE" by JOHN GLASWORTHY (From the Ambassadors Theatre London)
Saturday March 15th at 9.15 p.m.	"WHITE CARGO" by LEON GORDON (From the Playhouse Theatre London)
Sunday March 16th at 9.15 p.m.	JOURNEY'S END (LE GRAND VOYAGE) by R. C. SHERRIFF

PRICES OF ADMISSION

Baignoires...	P.T. 120	Orchestra Stalls P.T. 25	Balcony.......	P.T. 20
1st tier Boxes	» 80	Stalls A....... » 20	1st Gallery....	» 10
2nd tier Boxes	» 50	Stalls B....... » 15	2nd Gallery. .	» 5

Reduced prices for Military in uniform

Manager for Egypt: THOMAS SHAFTO

Handbill advertising Edward Stirling (Junior) and The English Players, in repertory at the Alhambra Theatre, Alexandria, Egypt, March 1930.

As I approach the conclusion of this introductory chapter, I want to mention one last example of British theatre from the pre-war period that owed its origins to the eighteenth century. This was the Stock Company and it was with one of these surviving companies that Richard Ward learnt his trade as a professional actor. Stock Company was the name given to a company of actors who, on a more or less permanent basis, were attached to or associated with one particular theatre or group of theatres. The first stock companies were those of the Drury Lane and Covent Garden in London. The stock companies were excellent training grounds for actors, especially young ones, in that company members were called upon to play a wide range of parts. Stock characters included 'Tragedian', 'Juvenile Lead' or 'General Utility'. These companies operated on a proper authentic repertory basis with a nightly change of repertory. One such company had been that formed and led by Edward Stirling [1809–84] and his wife Fanny [1809–94] whose productions consisted mostly of dramatisations of Dickens. It was with The Edward Stirling [Junior] Players that Ward gained his initial acting experience. This company enjoyed a huge commercial success in the nineteen twenties and thirties with a sensational melodrama in the context of 'The White Man's Burden', colonial Africa. Along with the plays of Coward and Lonsdale and farces of Ben Travers, it aptly represents the range and type of popular commercial theatre in this period. The production, *White Cargo*, by Leon Gordon, enjoyed long runs in both London and New York in addition to touring internationally. A company handbill [see opposite] reveals a repertory that might best be described as eclectic, changing every night and ranging from *White Cargo* through *Journey's End* to *The Importance of Being Earnest*.

In the ensuing chapters of this book, I shall be examining each of the four companies individually, but inevitably cross-referencing from time to time, as their aims and even personnel interacted and exchanged. Martin Browne was, I believe, motivated by a liberal social conscience as well as a profound Anglo-Catholic religious conviction. Ward, Harrison and Crockett were all, individually, active members at one stage or another of groups and movements such as the Independent Labour Party, the Peace Pledge Union, the Fellowship of Reconciliation and the Communist Party. In different ways, therefore, and to an extent determined by their own personal ethical or political temperament, they and their companies combined something, I believe, of the idealism and ethos of the Popular Front and liberal/left consensus of the pre-war period. Most significantly, with the exception of Browne, they were each Conscientious Objectors. Their combination of idealism, commitment to a more progressive, dedicated theatre and, equally important, their pragmatism is well expressed in the following quotation from Ward, written retrospectively in 1947:

> The Adelphi Players were never a specifically 'pacifist' company ... and propaganda was certainly never a part of their purpose Nevertheless, the majority of the company's early members were conscientious objectors who found in it the

opportunity to make a creative response to the war ... It may be asked what we felt to be behind the work, what principles and ideals motivated us? No doubt we had ideals of a kind; but I think we were a good deal more aware of certain practical facts; the need to earn our bread and butter in wartime, the difficulty of putting on a good performance in an air raid shelter and so forth. We wanted to be of use to the society in which we found ourselves by taking to ordinary men and women anywhere plays and performance of the highest quality we could achieve. [33]

33. R H Ward, 'The Adelphi Players: A Tabloid History', *Peace News*, 22 August 1947, p.4.

2

THE PILGRIM PLAYERS

The Pilgrim Players were formed in the early months of the war by E Martin Browne along with his wife, Henzie. The circumstances in which the original idea for the company emerged are described by her in the following extract from her memoirs of that period, *Pilgrim Story*:

> We went to Malvern ... and called on Allardyce Nicoll and his wife at their cottaqe overlooking the Malvern Hills ... We talked, of course, of the theatre both here and in America, where Allardyce was head of the Drama department at Yale; and one sentence stuck. Mrs Nicol, talking to Martin of the religious plays which were his particular interest, said in her sudden, dramatic way: "Take them round the country in a wagon!" We all laughed for it seemed so remote from immediate possibility. [1]

Martin Browne had then been taken quite seriously ill with jaundice. However, as he recovered, the idea of a travelling company of actors touring war-ravaged England began to take on clearer form:

> With returning health, ideas began to crystallise in Martin's mind. Thousands of people were going to be deprived of their recreation, just when they needed it. A small company should be formed to take the theatre to them. He had always felt that the link between the contemporary theatre and its audience was too tenuous. Now, in time of common trouble, actors and audiences exchanged experiences. Plague sent Shakespeare to inn-yards, banqueting halls, the village green ... should we go there, taking conditions in Britain as we found them? [2]

It is doubtful whether the Pilgrim Players would ever have been formed except for the circumstances of those early months of the war, that provoked this idealistic response of using theatre in a restorative sense in a time of political and social crisis. Such an initiative is characteristic of an uncomplicated, assumed patriotism that, whilst perhaps more prevalent and understandable then, resonates discordantly from our current, retrospective view. The cynical manipulation of such patriotic sentiments in the interests of political propaganda, for example in the Falklands and Gulf Wars, inevitably results in a more sceptical reading of such matters. The humorous,

---

1.   Henzie Browne, *Pilgrim Story* (London, Ferederick Muller, 1945), p.2.
2.   Ibid, p.4.

if sentimentalised, recollections of wartime Britain, particularly immediately post-Dunkirk, that were evoked by the popular television series 'Dad's Army' receive some substance in the following description. Henzie Browne is describing the difficulties that the company faced when setting out on its first tour of the South Coast. Their first tour coincided with the British retreat from Dunkirk:

> Every mile or two we were stopped by a road-block. Most of them were guarded, but the guards were not in uniform; they were farm labourers or clerks, all sorts ... Driving was nervous work, for there was no warning of any obstruction. One might come round a corner and find a barrier in front of the bonnet. What was more, it might be made of anything you could or could not think of ... most fantastic of all, bathing-boxes, still in their striped paint ... How long would these pathetic barriers delay a tank? The eleventh hour had struck for England, and her coast was defended by bathing-boxes! [3]

Throughout their existence as a touring company, the Pilgrim Players were to encounter such everyday difficulties and examples of the exigencies of wartime England.

Unlike The Adelphi Players who are discussed in the following chapter, the Pilgrim Players had no underlying concept of theatre associated with their work. Whereas R H Ward had written his manifesto article 'Theatre of Persons' as an expression of his aims for theatre, Martin Browne did not seek to elaborate any theoretical basis for his work. Neither did he see himself, as did Ward, as being at odds with the theatre establishment or as an instrument for radical change within the theatre. Interestingly, Ward had been a member of the early Pilgrim company, along with Phoebe Waterfield, who was to become one of the principal actresses with his Adelphi Players. Ward was rather critical of the absence of a more radical agenda in Browne's work as the following quotation from Adelphi Company Meeting minutes reveals:

> He [Ward] did not feel that the Pilgrim Players were a truly revolutionary movement in the theatre, because they appeared merely to be taking the old theatrical technique into new surroundings. The Pilgrims were, in fact, endeavouring to rehabilitate the old. [4]

The extent to which I believe these criticisms were justified I shall discuss later in this chapter. As we shall see, although Ward saw himself and his company as exponents of a more radical form of religious drama, he would not have subscribed to the more orthodox convictions of Martin Browne, either in themselves or in relation to theatre practice.

---

3.   Ibid, p.7.
4.   Richard Ward, cited in the minutes of The Adelphi Players Company Meeting, January, 1942.

Returning to Henzie Browne's account of the conception of the company, she recalls:

> Ideas kept on forming. Food rationing had begun. Food: bread. "Man cannot live by bread alone" ... We would do religious plays ... They could and should include comedy and farce, as well as suitable plays from the old mysteries and their modern counterparts and liturgical plays to be done in church. Thus every type of audience could share in the repertory. [5]

From the evidence of this statement one can clearly see the essentially reactionary and conservative basis for the company's work. Martin Browne's concepts of God and religion are contextualised unequivocally within patriarchal orthodoxy. In this important respect he shared common ground with his life-long friend Eliot. Nevertheless, as a corrective counterbalance, as I discussed in my introductory chapter, the wider initiative of Bishop George Bell in seeking to develop religious drama emerged out of his own hard-fought liberal presence within the Anglican establishment. Whilst Browne recognised the opportunity and need for a diversity of plays within the repertory, the assumption seems to be that they will all serve to make an implicit proselytism palatable to differing audiences. Whatever reservations one might have regarding this combination of prescriptive religious belief and theatre practice, it is clear that the major, twin motivating principles behind the work of the Pilgrim Players were as follows. Firstly, there was a recognition of the common human need that existed under the stress of wartime conditions for entertainment and cultural recreation. Secondly, there was Browne's associated conviction that providing that form of cultural enrichment might be allied to serving peoples' religious needs. This is not to presume that the aim or function of the Pilgrim Players was to 'evangelise' in terms of either the crude 'tele-evangelisation' of a simplistic, fundamentalist theology, nor in the narrowly historical Protestant sense of that term. Rather, to quote briefly from the stated aims of RADIUS: the Religious Drama Society of Great Britain (of which more will be said later in this chapter), Martin Browne sought to:

> ... encourage drama which illuminates the human condition. It aims to help local Christian congregations and creative groups to a deeper understanding of all types of drama. [6]

In terms of Elliott Martin Browne's pre-war reputation in the field of professional, religious drama, especially in relation to Eliot's verse plays, it is interesting to note that he had no formal, professional training in theatre.

---

5. Henzie Browne, p.2.
6. Quoted in the published aims and objectives of RADIUS: the Religious Drama Society of Great Britain, (Radius, 1990).

Apart from a brief spell with OUDS, the Oxford University Dramatic Society, he had not had any experience of either acting or directing. Martin Browne came from an Edwardian, solidly upper middle-class background. He had shown a passionate interest and commitment to the church, in this case the Anglo-Catholic tradition, from a relatively young age. He also began to develop a strong interest in theatre:

> I had still seen very few plays [Browne writing retrospectively of his situation as a young man of twenty-one years] but one of them was Barker's 'Dream', in 1914 ... the magic it left in my memory was that of brilliant light: such shining contrasts between the clearly defined life of the court and the mysterious shimmer of the woodland. The poetry was spoken fast and with agile expressiveness ... The only production that had a contemporary effect upon its contemporaries is another 'Dream', Peter Brook's of 1970. [7]

Martin Browne evidently had a keen appreciation of performance and production qualities. Nevertheless, as important and meaningful as that interest in theatre was, it was religion that was always, ultimately, to shape his beliefs, values and work. In the following passage, he refers tellingly to the crucial relationship that was to exist between the two throughout his life:

> My mind is cast in a sacramental mould, looking for 'the outward and visible sign of an inward and spiritual grace', needing the specific action to express the impulse of faith. So when I found anglo-catholic worship ... I realised that it helped to bring out also another latent power in me. The Eucharist is an action ... and it is action in a ritual form. I was deeply attracted by catholic ritual, and simultaneously by another kind of ritual that grew out of religion, the theatre. It was strange since I had no theatrical forbears. [8]

After successfully taking Honours in Theology at Oxford, Browne was determined that his future work would take him beyond the narrow confines of private pietism and academic seminars. He was concerned to enter into a kind of interventionist social work, specifically committing himself to particular working-class communities in the larger urban and industrial conurbations of London, the Midlands and the North. Like some others of his class, generation and theological persuasion, he held to a strong conviction that his religious beliefs should be demonstrated through achieving necessary social and political reforms. In Browne's case, his political impulses were characteristically and primarily 'pre-war Liberal'. This was in line with his class upbringing, with reforms emerging and being implemented within an essentially established and continuing social and economic order. Therefore,

---

7.   E Martin Browne with Henzie Browne, *Two in One*, (Cambridge University Press, 1981), p.6.
8.   Martin Browne, p.6.

on graduating, he joined an Educational Settlement as a staff member. The Workers' Educational Associations grew out of these Settlements and the majority of the funding came from prosperous, philanthropic families such as the Cadburies and Rowntrees. Martin Browne recollected his initial impressions of that period in his life:

> I saw politically for the first time. Then I saw socially: ... a Baptist minister called Brown ... had a settlement in Hull, and I then went to Liverpool, then to York ... [which was] for me a potent mixture of back-to-back housing and soaring Minster. [9]

As he prepared to join the staff of the York settlement, his involvement in theatre grew steadily and he became close friends with Robert Speaight, who was to become recognised as one of the most distinguished actors of his generation. Speaight went on to play, amongst many other famous roles, the part of Beckett in the premiere of *Murder in the Cathedral*. There is an interesting reference to the ideas and practice of William Poel which Browne, along with Ward, were to recall when facing the demands of performing plays in spartan conditions in the war years:

> Most of our [Browne and Speaight] talk was of Shakespeare ... Constantly on our lips was the name of William Poel, the crusader who dragged the theatre back from its obsession with scenery to the actual texts of the plays and their unbroken continuity. We revered him, with Barker, Robert Atkins at the Old Vic and Bridges-Adams at Stratford as his disciples. [10]

Robert Atkins of course, was to go on to establish and provide theatre to a wider public through his legendary productions of Shakespeare in the open-air theatre in Regent's Park. Indeed, he was to present Shakespeare during the height of the Blitz in October 1940 at the Vaudeville Theatre. Norman Marshall offers an assessment of Atkins' work at the Old Vic, where he had been the first producer after the 1914–18 war:

> Atkins adopted a method of production similar to that which Bridges-Adams inaugurated at Stratford about the same time. He concentrated on speed and simplicity. Scenery was cut down to a minimum in order to facilitate quick changes. [11]

Suffice to say that the work of innovators such as Poel, Monck, Atkins, Granville-Barker and Bridges-Adams influenced a whole generation of directors.

---

9. Ibid, p.11.
10. Ibid, p.12.
11. Norman Marshall, *The Other Theatre*, (London, John Lehmann, 1947), p.129.

Through his friendship with Speaight, Martin Browne was invited to participate in a prestigious amateur summer theatre festival at Angmering-on-Sea on the Sussex coast, prior to starting his work at York. It was there in 1924 that he met the young actress, Henzie Raeburn, who was soon after to become his wife. Raeburn had trained professionally as an actress and had already had the opportunity of working with directors such as the Russian emigre, Komisarjevsky and Granville-Barker. At this time, It was quite common for professional actors and directors to be invited to 'guest' at festivals like that at Angmering, where Raeburn played Ophelia to Martin Browne's Horatio. They married that winter and the couple became established at a Doncaster settlement. It is arguable that it was through her influence that the couple made a specific decision to include theatre in their outreach work at Doncaster and elsewhere. This theatre ranged from a simple production of a candle-lit Mystery Play in a church, through to a production, encouraged by their close friend, Sybil Thorndike, of Toller's expressionistic *Masses and Man*:

> This was vibrant theatre ... but comprehensible to anybody in an area of industrial turmoil ... For [the character of] 'the Nameless' we had an active Communist ... a widely read man whom the Party had ordered to stay at the coalface rather than climb the educational ladder because he could 'do more good there'. [12]

This anecdotal account of their theatre work amongst working-class communities in the north of England encapsulates some of the issues that I raised in my previous chapter: for example, the eclectic range of theatre being produced outside of conventional frames of venues and audiences. The presence of an active Communist in the cast reminds one of the work of the WTM in this period.

After their production of Toller's play in Doncaster, the Brownes organised and produced, at the invitation of the Governor, a production of the *Coventry Mystery Nativity Play* at Wakefield Prison. They had established good working relationships within the working-class community whom they lived and worked amongst. However, in 1926, the year of The General Strike, they were required to leave their work in the north.

> ... after the abandonment [of The General Strike] they [the miners] were left to carry on alone. We saw privation steadily overtake them ... Soon food was getting short. It was clear that The Folkhouse [the name given to the settlement] could not survive after five month's strike ... the youngest of the educational settlements was doomed. We must look for other work. [13]

---

12. Martin Browne, p.34.
13. Ibid, p.37.

The limitations, and even contradictions, raised in this kind of liberal, progressive enterprise are important. In the context of major social and political unrest such as The General Strike, such initiatives ceased and the communities, effectively, abandoned. In identifying the paternalistic benevolence of such projects, I simultaneously believe that such projects only served to ameliorate the visible symptoms of a wider political and economic malaise. For the couple, there then followed temporary work with the British Drama League, founded in 1919, as adjudicators for their Festivals of Community Drama. Elliott Martin Browne also gained his first opportunity, with the Stage Society, of professional acting work in their production of D H Lawrence's *David*, a play that was to become part of the Pilgrim repertory, and which I shall discuss later in this chapter. Then, through the help of a family friend, the playwright John van Druten, Martin Browne accepted an invitation to teach Drama at Carnegie College in the United States of America.

RADIUS and *Murder in the Cathedral*

It was whilst on a brief holiday back in England that Browne was approached by Bishop George Bell. About to leave his diocese of Winchester and take up his responsibilities as Bishop of Chichester, he invited Martin Browne to accept the inaugural post of Director of Religious Drama in the diocese. This post was not as safely respectable as it might appear from our contemporary viewpoint. There was still a strong residue of Puritan thinking in the wider Anglican establishment that religious drama was, at best, superfluous, and, at worst, too close to secular modernity. As I outlined in my introduction, Bell played a significant role in trying to bridge links between the arts and religion. In 1928, Bell had arranged for a Nativity Play to be performed in the nave of Canterbury Cathedral, possibly the first time that a dramatic performance had occured inside an Anglican church since the medieval period. In 1929, Bell invited Nugent Monck to bring his Maddermarket Players from Norwich to perform *Everyman* and *Dr Faustus* in the Chapter House at Canterbury. [14] This event carried with it a special significance in that it effectively inaugurated the Canterbury Festival, of which *Murder in the Cathedral* was to be its most distinguished and enduring achievement. A decision had been taken in the early development of this festival that only new commissioned works from contemporary dramatists should be produced. Laurence Binyon's *The Young King* (1934) would precede Eliot's play the following year which itself was followed by Dorothy Sayers' *The Zeal of the House* in 1937. Returning to the earlier stages of Bell's plans, he founded RADIUS: the Religious Drama Society of Great Britain, in 1930. Bell became its first President, with Sybil Thorndike its Vice-President. As in the work going on in the settlements, the emergence of the Religious Drama

---

14. Browne, citing Ronald Jasper's *George Bell* (Oxford, 1967).

Society represented a similar middle-class initiative in encouraging the development of drama within churches. As I discussed in my opening chapter, the numbers of people attending churches had continued to fall rapidly in the first part of the twentieth century. Therefore the use of drama to raise awareness of religion within an increasingly secularised and polarised society was viewed as crual to reformers such as Bell. The re-emergence of the religious drama movement had wider sources of course, and was evident in both the experimental verse plays of Yeats, and also in his efforts with the actress Margot Collis, to form a poets' theatre. Laurence Housman, D H Lawrence and John Masefield had also experimented in the writing of religious plays. Housman's *Abraham and Isaac* became a popular choice in the early Adelphi repertory whilst, as I have already noted, *David* became a rather less successful part of the Pilgrim's repertory. The final pragmatic piece in the jigsaw of the genre's revival was Ashley Dukes who, as a shrewd businessman and entrepreneur, provided the theatrical business-sense to ensure that plays such as Eliot's *Murder in the Cathedral* would be seen by wider audiences in the secular, commercial theatre, beyond the cloistered confines of Canterbury. The following observations by Sidnell cleverly focus attention on the intermarriage between the secular and the religious in the drama of the thirties:

> Throughout the thirties, the interplay of theatrical technique with political or religious ideas was often bewildering ... Was ensemble acting a Socialist method or an apolitical technique? ... Did parable and doggerel point to the Left, symbolism and poetry to the Right? ... Why did nobody speak of religious or poetic theatre, or, conversely, of workers, or political drama? [15]

I think it is quite clear to see how Martin Browne's eventual work with the Pilgrim Players and, of course, his pre-war work as both the first professional Religious Drama Advisor and the director of Eliot's plays, arose out of and reflected these important aspects of British social and cultural life in the late twenties and thirties. Browne had seen the potentially positive results that theatre could achieve in undertakings such as the WEA settlements and so, whilst the new post of Drama Advisor meant a considerable drop in salary from his work at Carnegie, he was persuaded to take up his new post in the summer of 1930.

Just before this decision was taken, Browne and his wife had taken a short holiday to see the Passion Play at Oberammergau. Their disappointed reaction to it as religious drama throws further light upon their developing views of what constituted good theatre and, implicitly, religious drama:

---

15. Michael Sidnell, *Dances of Death: The Group Theatre of London in the Thirties* (London, Faber and Faber, 1984), p.25.

It was only at a few moments, such as the washing of the disciple's feet, that a surge of emotion occurred. For the most part, the strength one had felt in the church was regimented into a pious conformity. I was rebelliously determined to get away from this pietism in the work ahead of me ... it must be free to grow into our own century, free to find its own life. [16]

Whilst they began their work in Chichester, another experience of theatre had a much more stimulating and inspiring effect upon Browne. This was a performance in London by Michel Saint-Denis and Copeau's La Compagnie des Quinze, with Browne being particularly impressed by the sparse, clean and vivid ensemble work of the company. The work of Copeau and his nephew and collaborator, Saint-Denis, was to prove influential within British progressive theatre in the nineteen thirties and forties. After the company disbanded, Saint-Denis decided to settle In London and in 1935 directed Gielgud in a translation of Obey's *Noah* which was later to become part of the Adelphi repertory.

Meanwhile, in his new role as Drama Advisor, Browne discovered – not surprisingly – that the quality of the work that was being presented in parishes was often what the Americans call "bathrobe drama", which may be translated, according to Browne, into an English context as, "dressing-gown Palestinian". [17]

Apart from the obvious and painful lack of experience and professional expertise to be found in the average parish church, Browne – with Bell's full support – recognised the pressing need for professional writers working within a sympathetic context to that of his own aims and beliefs. Whilst there was the work of the two French disciples of Copeau, Obey and Ghéon [18] there were few, if any, playwrights of a comparable quality and vision working within England:

Up to now, almost all of the plays available, even those of quality, operated within the accepted framework: they were celebratory rather than exploratory. If our drama was to speak to our own time we must find fresh voices. [19]

---

16. Martin Browne, p.58.
17. Ibid, p.70.
18. Jacques Copeau (1879–1949) was a major influence on the development of modern French theatre. An actor, director and playwright, he formed his own theatre company, the Vieux-Colombier, which launched his quest for an actor-centred form of physical theatre, combining the aesthetic with the ethical and religious.

André Obey (1892–1975) was a French playwright closely associated with Copeau's company, whose company commissioned and staged five of his plays. His work was introduced to this country primarily through Copeau's nephew, the outstanding actor and director Michel Saint-Denis. Henri Ghéon (1875–1943) was a French dramatist influential in the revival of religious verse drama. Like his compatriot, Obey, his work was produced by Copeau amongst others.
19. Martin Browne, p.93

Thus it was in October 1932 that Bell called a week-end conference at which he invited interested and active professional theatre practitioners to try and establish the next direction for the development of religious drama. In its way, it was to prove to be an important meeting with far-reaching consequences and implications. Whilst he was not able to attend this conference, the writer who was not only one of the foremost poets of his generation and, indeed, the century, had already been approached by Bell. Simultaneously, Bell arranged the initial meeting between the Brownes and Eliot which was to lead to a life long friendship. It was not to be until 1933, however, that Martin Browne and Eliot were to begin their professional relationship. Browne showed himself to be a director with a heightened sense and appreciation of Eliot's dramatic verse.

However, he was also aware of the need for the verse to function as a theatrical language. Eliot himself was keen to explore further the potential for verse drama following the relative success of The Group Theatre's production of *Sweeney Agonistes*. He was delighted therefore to meet, in Browne, someone who saw the challenge of developing an effectively new form of theatrical language:

> Eliot had always been concerned with the possibility of an acceptable poetic drama ... The problem was to find a form of drama and a concomitant form of verse ... where the poetry was neither out of place nor a mere decoration, but was felt as intrinsic to the realisation of a poetic quality inherent in the vision of the play. [20]

Eliot had been in discussions with both Doone and Dukes regarding a season of his own and Yeats' plays at the Mercury Theatre. Doone, naturally, hoped that the season of plays would be produced by The Group at the Mercury under the entrepreneurial management of Dukes. However, the discussions ended acrimoniously. Dukes, however, did succeed in getting the professional rights for Eliot's play. The premiere of *Murder in the Cathedral* was in the Chapter House of Canterbury Cathedral in June 1935. Whilst one critic, Conrad Aiken, said of the opening night: "... One hadn't listened two minutes before one felt that one was witnessing a play which had the quality of greatness ..." [21], the premiere went largely unnoticed. Glenda Leeming discusses that opening production in the context of the Chapter House as a converted and adapted venue:

> The first production ... impressed audiences far beyond the cultural endurance that Eliot modestly suggested as their motive. The chapter house stage, specially built, was shallow and had no exits, so that actors came and went through the audience or had to stay on stage. Against the rhythmic shapes of the arcading

---

20. Tolley, p.186
21. Cited in Martin Browne, p.94.

with its painted decoration in 'cold colours' the actors stood out through their vivid costumes – the monks in Benedictine robes of black, the tempters in yellow, the chorus in green with red and blue patterns. [22]

Ashley Dukes saw the commercial viability potential in the play. He had opened the Mercury, a converted chapel in Notting Hill Gate, in 1931 as the base for his wife's Ballet Rambert company. Run as a Ballet School, this arrangement covered the payment of the general overheads and meant that, following its licence as a theatre in 1933, Dukes was able to take commercial risks that otherwise might have proved impossible. Dukes took the production, with an entirely professional cast, to the Mercury, where it ran for a hundred performances until 23 February 1936. The production was seen by some twenty thousand people during its initial run. It transferred from the Mercury to the Duchess Theatre in the West End and also played at the Old Vic. In all, it ran for eight hundred performances in London between November 1935 and March 1938. In the original Canterbury production, Martin Browne himself played the Fourth Tempter whilst Phoebe Waterfield and Nina Evans both featured in the chorus of *The Women of Canterbury*. Whilst Waterfield was to be a long-standing actress with the Adelphi Players, both of the young actresses worked, for a time, with the Pilgrim Players. Robert Speaight said of his portrayal of Beckett: 'It was true that Beckett was an idea rather than a character, but there was a strong challenge in clothing the idea with flesh and blood. [23]

In 1938, following its London success, the production was taken to America. The late Pamela Keily, whom I had the privilege to meet before her death in 1984, was a young actress in 1938 and not long from her training at RADA. She was invited to join the cast for the American production. This was to represent the beginning of a life-long commitment to the development of religious drama in many parishes – in factory workplaces as well as churches – throughout post-war Britain. In her memoirs, she recounted the journey out to America:

> It was January 1938 when we were due to play at Liverpool before sailing to Boston ... Ten days at sea, most of us sick at the start, eventually landed in USA – with a further ten days of rehearsal before the first night in Boston amidst a horde of T S Eliot's relatives. Christopher Casson got appendicitis the moment we landed and had to have an operation. Sybil Thorndike was playing in 'Time and the Conways' in New York and ... arrived to look after her youngest son and watch him cling to the scenery on our first night in New York. [24]

---

22. Glenda Leeming, *Poetic Drama* (Macmillan, 1989), p.83.
23. Robert Speaight, 'Interpreting Beckett and Other Parts, in *T S Eliot: A Symposium for his Seventieth Birthday*, edited by Neville Braybrooke (Rupert Hart Davies, 1958), p.71.
24. Pamela Keily, *Memoirs*, edited by Kay Hudson and Kenneth Payne, (Otley, Smith Settle, 1986), p.12.

Although the production played to disappointing audiences, it received excellent reviews in the American press:

> ... a rare and beautiful play, unconventional in form, imaginatively staged, ably acted ... [25]

> ... highly imaginative and filled with a sense of the catharsis of pure tragedy ... Eliot proves himself a man of the theater as well as a poet ... the role of Beckett is interpreted with unusual power by Robert Speaight [whose] Beckett is a man of humanity as well as of heroic stature. [26]

With, finally, Brooks Atkinson observing the *The New York Times*:

> ... It is a sublime bit of dramatic transfiguration; and Speaight speaks it with a religious passion and a personal humility that are deeply moving ... [27]

It was on their return from the foreshortened American tour that Martin Browne and his wife found themselves in the circumstances that opened this chapter.

Following on further success between Eliot and Browne with the production of *The Family Reunion* in March 1939, the Brownes spent the fateful summer prior to September of that year at the Tewkesbury Festival. This was a festival, along the lines of Canterbury, for which Browne was the Festival Director.

> War got closer and closer and there was only a week before all theatres were closed ... It was in the enormous upheaval of life that Martin conceived the first of the 'suitcase rackets', a term that covered an effort to take the theatre to the evacuated population. [28]

After the heady atmosphere, successes and elation of Canterbury, the West End and New York, they were to find themselves drawn back to the people and parishes reminiscent of their earlier years in Sussex and in the settlements.

The Pilgrim Players: Early Stages

Following the circumstances and conditions under which the original idea for the Pilgrim Players emerged, Martin and Henzie Browne then faced the practicalities of how to assemble a company, find a base, and secure a means of transport, in order to take theatre out to the people. They obviously had a strong link with Canterbury and it was there that they were invited to establish

---

25. Elliot Norton, 'Rare Drama Presented at Schubert', *Boston Times*, 1 February 1938, p.4.
26. Elinor Hughes, *Murder in the Cathedral*, 1 February 1938.
27. Brooks Atkinson, *New York Times*, 1 February 1938, p.3.
28. Keily, p.13.

a temporary base for their family and their work. The Headmaster of Kent College, a private school in Canterbury, invited the Brownes to stay at the school. In return for some small teaching duties, they had a relatively secure and safe home as well as rehearsal facilities for the, as yet, uncast company. It was shortly after this time in the early months of the Pilgrim Player's existence that Browne wrote to Eliot from Benenden School in Kent requesting:

> Whether we could possibly do an emergency version of 'Murder in the Cathedral'? The company is 5 men and 4 women ... It would frankly be an emergency version and billed as such: it would enable us to present the play in a lot of places where it will never otherwise be seen ... and I badly want some Eliot in our repertory ... We are here till the 31st May [1940] and then go to Dorset on a strenuous tour. At present people are carrying on with bookings and we hope to keep alive, especially going Westwards. But who can tell? [29]

Eliot agreed readily to their request. Having secured an initial touring and rehearsal base and the promise of an adapted Eliot for their repertory, they then chose upon the name of the Canterbury Pilgrim Players. The inclusion of the city name was to distinguish them from a similar company that was hoping to operate out of Oxford. Founded by Ruth Spalding, who had been a traveling producer for RADIUS before the war, the Oxford Pilgrims toured for the early part of the war. Both Richard Ward and Phoebe Waterfield appeared in her production of Charles Williams' *Terror of Light*. The fundamental question remained of recruiting a company to work with in their pioneering work. Obviously many who might have joined were already being conscripted into the Armed Services. However, they were able to assemble together a small group of professional actors and others whose experience was more limited. All of the male actors were Conscientious Objectors, amongst whom were those who were Pacifists. The tribunals allowed that they could fulfil their non-combatant War Work within the company. I will discuss these issues in more detail in the following chapter. Nearly two years after the company had started its touring work, Browne was able to report, in July 1941, in a letter to Eliot that:

> We have been lucky enough to remain unchanged in personnel for all this time. I doubt whether the lull will continue for much longer, though there is a sort of 'reserved occupation' label attaching to the Players in some quarters and we may be left alone. It certainly would be good for the quality of the work, and enables us to do far more than when we had to continually rehearse new people. [30]

Amongst those company members were Nina Evans and Pamela Keily along with two brothers, Brian and Denis Carey, who had had substantial experience

---

29. E Martin Browne, *The Making of T S Eliot's Plays*, (Cambridge University Press, 1969), pp.153–4).
30. Ibid, p.155.

with the Abbey and Gate theatres in Dublin prior to the war. The company
were to enjoy almost eighteen months of unbroken consistency. The company
members, at the suggestion of Martin Browne, agreed to be paid a common
basic salary which they called the 'Tommy Rate': thirty shillings a week, the
same rate as the ordinary 'Tommy' or infantryman. All assets were to be
held in common, which, as will be evident in the following chapters, was
also an important characteristic of the Adelphi and Compass Players.
Allocation of monies for shoe repairs, stamps and even cod liver oil tablets
was democratically discussed at the regular Company Meetings.

Tobias and the Angel by James Bridie [31] was to be the first hastily rehearsed
production, the author giving special permission, like Eliot, for an 'emergency'
version to be performed:

> It [the project itself and the 'Tommy Rate'] was a mad idea perhaps, though Actors'
> Equity was willing to give it provisional approval. A lot of actors naturally thought
> it was too quixotic even for wartime ... At last, however, we were complete and
> rehearsals began in the hall, papier-mache was being made in the drawing-room,
> in fact Kent College was inundated with preparations for the first performance. [32]

In a letter written late in 1939 and sent from their Kent headquarters, Martin
Browne invited Eliot to join the Patrons of the new company:

> The other [Patrons] will be:
> The Archbishop of Canterbury [Cosmo Lang]
> Bishop of Chichester
> John Gielgud
> Sybil Thorndike
> Marie Tempest
>
> We start next week and have a good company and keen, lots of bookings, with
> 'Tobias' followed by the Wakefield Shepherds-cum-Charles Williams Nativity
> programme. [33]

East Kent was a reception area for the many hundreds of children that were
being evacuated from the capital. Therefore, many of the first performances
were to children and their supervising adults housed in the many schools
and church halls in that area. The following extract indicates some of the
conditions that the company frequently found themselves performing under:

---

31. James Bridie (1888–1951) was the pseudonym for Osborne Henry Mavor, a Scottish doctor
turned playwright who was a co-founder of the Glasgow Citizen's Theatre. His work is
characterised by a light, lyrical style, poetic and resonant at its best in plays such as *Mr Bolfry*
(1943) a favourite with the Adelphi companies.
32. Martin Browne, p.118.
33. Browne, *T S Eliot's Plays*, p.152.

On our first circular we had offered 'performances anytime, anywhere'. We were fulfilling the slogan. One of the reasons for it was the lack of shelters ... till shelters were built the numbers allowed at any assembly were restricted in all schools and in the coast towns: so relay performances were the only way of giving everyone a chance. Consequently, 9.15. one wintry morning saw us playing in a classroom in Ramsgate, with the children banked upon the desks in order of height, and the play given on the floor in front of a screen which formed the only entrance and the only setting. At the village hut, Wychling, there were no dressing rooms. The girls had two feet of wing space, the men a bell-tent in the field outside ... Oil lamps for lighting were frequent; and low prosceniums would sometimes decapitate the Angel. [34]

In those early days and months the company were relying upon the Browne's small family car for transport and they were not always helped by the weather:

On 16 January the severest snowstorm of the winter fell. We were due to play ... at Elvington, a mining village on the heights above Dover. The actors were put on the train. Martin, driving out with the little car with the costumes and properties, lost his way in the blizzard and was fairly stuck in a snowdrift. He got out by going into reverse and then driving off the road into the neighbouring ploughed field ... With a spade borrowed from a near-by cottage, the car was finally dug out and finally got to Elvington. Any time, any place, any weather! [35]

Companies such as the Pilgrims, Adelphis and Compass were always going to face the constant challenge of difficult conditions and meagre resources. Martin Browne was to recall nearly forty years later:

Our ... battle was to maintain our standard and gradually to raise it, in face of great odds. Lewis Casson once said, when he visited us on tour, "Your danger is that for you the acting is the rest". [36]

Nevertheless, what characterises all of their work was the unswerving idealism that motivated and committed them, both to one another and to their audiences, scattered in small towns and villages around Britain. Many of these communities would never have encountered any form of live, professional theatre previously. In a sense they were building upon the work of pre-war enterprises such as the Arts League of Service. This was an organisation which emerged in 1919 as a means of uniting practitioners in the arts – usually with broadly 'progressive' convictions or sympathies – in an attempt to utilise the arts as a means of countering the despair of the post-

---

34. Henzie Browne, p.119.
35 Ibid, p.121.
36. Martin Browne, p.137.

war years, and embodying a broadly humanist vision of rebuilding a better world. As Eleanor Elder, an actress with one of touring Arts League theatre groups, recalled in her account of their work:

> The story of the Arts League of Service Travelling Theatre begins in that post-war period of released tension, when so many fine ideas of social reconstruction were finding expression ... the benefits ... of education, culture and art were to be shared by all. [37]

This idealistic conviction of the restorative power and potential of the arts resurfaces continually through the work of the companies under consideration. It is important to remember that, under the conditions of war, the need for restorative and recreational cultural activities was particularly felt. In the context of the church and its own decline and problematic relationship to most ordinary people's lives:

> The war made matters worse than ever. A gloomy significance was read by the faithful into the silencing of the parish church bells. Another portent of the advance of secularism was the complacency with which ministers encouraged factories to work on Sundays. [38]

'Holding all things in Common': Company Structure and Function

As the company became more established during those early months, the Company Meeting became the central expression of that growing stability, and the accompanying need to formalise and rationalize the various decisions that had to be regularly made. The first recorded Minutes are dated 11 February 1940, and opened with a statement of the principles on which the company is run:

> The capital is administered co-operatively by the company. The artistic control and control of engagements are in the hands of the Director ... A grant of £150 per annum had been made by CEMA [the newly formed Council for the Encouragement of Music and the Arts] mainly for the purpose of increasing salaries. The possibility of giving the company a holiday on pay was discussed. [39]

The award of a grant by CEMA, the forerunner of the Arts Council, represents a significant precedent, in that the Pilgrims were the first ever theatre company to receive any form of financial subsidy from an official government source.

---

37. Eleanor Elder, *Travelling Players: The Story of the Arts League of Service* (London, Frederick Muller, 1939), p.l.
38. Angus Calder, *The People's War – Britain 1939–1945* (Jonathan Cape, 1969), p.479.
39. Martin Browne, p.123.

The Adelphi Players also received similar financial assistance shortly afterwards, although Ward was always suspicious of government funding, seeing in it the potential for control and compromise of artistic choice and integrity.

Whilst the amount of money seems small and insignificant by today's standard, this precedent of government intervention in, and financial support of, the arts represented the beginnings of a relationship between the State and the arts which continues to be debated and controversial. This has especially proved the case under the monetarist, market-economy-dominated decades of the nineteen eighties and nineties. At the time of writing, the controversies surrounding both the 'rationalisation' of the Arts Council itself and the parlous, inefficient, consumption of massive amounts of taxpayers money by the Royal Opera House, promise that this debate will continue throughout the new millenium.

Nevertheless, under the conditions of austerity and rationing that everyone faced during wartime, Martin Browne was understandably glad to receive the added security that the funding gave to the company. In as much as all members of the company received the common 'Tommy Rate', so all tasks within the company were also equally distributed. The Pilgrim Players represented a stimulating and diverse cross-section of people, motive and values. For many, if not quite all, of the company, there was a shared conviction to Conscientious Objection:

> Everyone believed in the work, but they came to that belief from divergent motives. There were Christians who wanted to offer Christian ideas through their art. There were agnostics who disapproved of the outspokenly Christian plays but felt that the theatre had a duty to the people ... There were Pacifists, who found a war service compatible with their conscience – and the tribunals agreed with them. And there were keen young women, and young men awaiting, or unfit for, military service, to whom this was the best theatrical experience available. [40]

Returning once more to the Company Meetings, they were run on quite formal lines and whilst Martin Browne had overall artistic control of the company, the role of chairperson for the meetings was elected on a monthly basis, usually alternating between a woman and a man. From the point at which CEMA became formally – i.e. financially – involved with the company, more stringent demands were made upon the formal accounting of finances, including both expenditure and box office receipts:

> Accounts had become more elaborate ... auditors and CEMA must be satisfied. It was hard to assess accurately what our weekly takings had been, as money for some shows did not come in for a month or two after they were played. But from

---

40. Ibid, p.136.

the time we turned northwards in September 1940 a steady rise in the box office was evident. When the south coast, threatened with invasion, had yielded us only £30 to £40 a week, the north, further from the war, produced half as much again. [41]

Like the Adelphi Players and the Compass Players, the Pilgrims only ever asked for a minimum guarantee to offset possible poor takings at any given venue. Furthermore these companies were always prepared to play at venues where it was not reasonable to expect any revenue, e.g. at prisons. However, it is interesting to note that the box office returns actually increased over the months which coincided with a marginally increased grant from CEMA. This meant that extras such as a clothing fund were set up:

> The fund's policy was exhaustively discussed at meetings ... When a member applied for an article the committee took great pains to price it in various shops before giving its grant. For instance, two Pilgrims needed new overcoats. After much research, £7 was voted to each. [42]

Unfortunately there is little other remaining documentary evidence of the content of these regular monthly meetings. Whilst there were inevitably disagreements, overall the company seems to have survived the stresses and strains of such hand-to-mouth-existence remarkably well. There is certainly no evidence of any major disputes over organisational or artistic matters. Nevertheless, such a life style was bound to take its toll as Pamela Keily recalled in later years:

> Black-outs, continuous changing of lodgings and the struggle to keep the work up to standard had the added strain of Martin's idealistic conception of 'holding all things in common' ... I realise now how the strain of wartime conditions and the inescapably close contact with some eight or nine theatrical temperaments probably made me intensely tiresome and distorted in outlook. It became clearly evident after two and a half years that I must move. [43]

Pamela Keily left the company on good terms and went on to what was to become a life time's commitment to the development of quality drama around the country. Her concept of religious drama was eclectic and liberal, probably more attuned in that sense to Ward rather than Browne. Part of this work involved her forming the Pilgrims who toured in the immediate post-war period. Towards the end of her career, she was rewarded with an MBE for her services to religious drama in the community. She also exercised influence through her recognition of the need to encourage and commission new writers such as Norman Nicholson and the young Alan Plater.

---

41. Ibid, pp. 137–8.
42. Ibid, p.138.
43. Keily, p.15.

She also commissioned Wilfred Harrison in the nineteen seventies to write *Coming of Age*, a definitive play about Dietrich Bonhoeffer which has been produced across the world, including the United States of America and Germany.

Returning to the structure of the Pilgrim Players, in conclusion it can be said that it reflected, for all of the inevitable stresses and frustrations, a concrete expression of Browne's assertion of 'holding all things in common'. As George Rowell observes:

> In their modest way the company displayed the 'Battle of Britain' spirit no less proudly than the magnificent 'small boat' Armada organised to rescue the Dunkirk survivors or the heroism of the 'First of the Few' fighter pilots. [44]

However, ideals and good-will would not have ensured their survival. One inevitably returns to the presence and involvement [Ward might have said 'interference'] of CEMA in ensuring the survival of the company. As Browne recalled:

> CEMA's help to us was not primarily financial. Our overheads were so infinitesimal that we could get along safely on a very small margin. But the Council established our bona-fides with government departments ... Only with this help could we have survived the increase in every kind of rationing and control ... however unusual we seemed to the more orthodox theatre men among its associates, the Council itself encouraged us to work out our own methods and was always patient with our blunderings. [45]

Touring and Repertory

In the following extract, Henzie Browne assesses the position of the company in Easter 1940, some few months after the hastily assembled company had been formed for their first production *Tobias and the Angel*:

> The company had increased to nine and acquired the members who were to be itss strength over the next three years ... Brian Carey became transport officer, which involved not only driving but petrol coupons, repairs, and the seating of the company, ensuring that each had a turn in front. By now we had two cars and a trailer for each; the job of loading these was a highly expert one calling for all the ingenuity of the Carey brothers. [46]

Annette Welby, secretary of the Religious Drama Society, had been advance manager for the company initially. For a very short period after Pamela Keily

---

44. George Rowell and Anthony Jackson, *The Repertory Movement: A History of Regional Theatre in Britain* (Cambridge University Press, 1984), p.77.
45. Martin Browne, p.140.
46. Henzie Browne, p.124.

had left the company she had also operated as advance agent for the company in Kent and Sussex. As with other similar enterprises, the Pilgrims relied heavily upon word of mouth advance publicity and also upon hospitality in terms of help with food and accomodation:

> A few days later we left London for a south-country tour. Our first billet was a mill [which] ground the finest wholemeal flour ... the bread was certainly delicious. But we found raw salads and baked potatoes left some gaps in the diet of busy people. For we were busy in those days. Two plays, and quite exacting ones, in our repertory, and a third being rehearsed; the diary shows ten and eleven performances a week, which means setting and striking stage eight or nine times, and driving hundreds of miles as well as playing and rehearsing. In the week of 3rd March twelve shows are recorded, including the first performance of Henri Gheon's 'The Way of the Cross.' [47]

Before considering in more detail some of their plays in repertory, it is worth reflecting upon the varied venues that they frequently found themselves performing in, ranging from Maidstone Gaol to Dartington Hall in Devon:

> During 1940 we played only a few single matinees in theatres – Brighton, Eastbourne, Folkestone – plus some longer visits to Little Theatres: the Questors at Ealing, the Civic at Bradford, the People's at Newcastle. [48]

As with the Adelphis, the Pilgrim Players were committed to playing any venue where there was a need or interest in their work. One of their venues in the early months, in fact on the day that Boulogne fell, was the barn theatre attached to Ellen Terry's Kent cottage; a production which was lit with two motor headlamps from the front row of the audience. Soon after this they performed at New Romney where the vicar had been unable to raise what was, by then, the guaranteed minimum fee of three guineas per show. The company performed anyway and took six guineas in receipts. They stayed at Dartington at the personal invitation of the Elmhirst family [49], the idea being that the company should rehearse their emergency version of *Murder in the Cathedral* for six weeks whilst going out into the surrounding countryside to take other plays from their repertory. Initially most of their touring had inevitably been in the South and West but as the bombing raids increased in severity in the industrialised towns of the North and Midlands, so there were increasing requests to perform in those areas. This was not however before they had been invited to play a week at the Arts Theatre

47. Ibid, p.123.
48. Martin Browne, p.142.
49. Leonard and Dorothy Elmhirst were a married couple, whose liberal values and philanthropy founded the Dartington School project at Dartington Hall near Totnes, Devon. They also, at the same base, funded the revival of local and traditional crafts.

Cambridge, receiving good reviews in the national press, including Ivor Brown of *The Observer*: "... one is naturally shy of giving particular praise where the temper of general teamwork is exemplary." [50]

The Pilgrims faced a considerable contrast when leaving the Arts Theatre in early 1941, to perform in the crowded air raid shelters of the industrialised cities with a very different type of audience:

> Our start in the shelters was made at Lloyd's in Leadenhall Street. The whole basement of the great building was fitted with bunks and held over two hundred sleepers ... I think that all who played that performance of 'Murder in the Cathedral' will always remember it; and most of the audience will too ... Before dressing as Beckett, Martin gave a short talk about the play, and then went through it without a break. [51]

The following two short references from Angus Calder's excellent *The People's War* help to capture something of the mood within the shelters at this stage in the war:

> A hymn composed and circulated widely during the Blitz began: God is our refuge, be not afraid, He will be with you all through the raid. [52]

whilst:

> In London in 1940, the inhabitants of one shelter so much enjoyed a recording of 'The Magic Flute' in German that it was repeated the next night. But in Bristol in 1943, one resident wrote to the local paper complaining that ... the BBC had broadcast 'over a hundred and twenty' programmes featuring German music during the previous six weeks. [53]

The Pilgrims also found themselves in demand at various Forces Bases, including those in the northernmost Highlands of Scotland where at one base, the servicemen had actually built a foot-high stage, a row of footlights and a dressing room:

> It was [their] pride and joy; but it was only eight feet by six feet, so we got dressed in relays, the others remaining outside until it got too cold ... The audience of seventy packed the hut, and they were good enough to refrain from smoking lest we should be choked, as there was no ventilation. [54]

---

50. Ivor Browne, *The Observer*, cited in Henzie Browne, p.142.
51. Martin and Henzie Browne, pp.143–44.
52. Calder, p.480.
53. Ibid, p.489.
54. Henzie Browne, p.123.

Whilst much of the evidence concerning touring conditions and venues is inevitably anecdotal, to my mind, it serves once more to communicate the atmosphere of that period and to highlight the unique and invaluable work that companies such as the Pilgrims and Adelphis carried out during those war years. In the following section, I intend to examine three of the plays from the repertory and to consider the extent to which the religious dimension to the Pilgrim's work affected their choice of plays in repertory.

Three Plays In Repertory

In an attempt to deal concisely with relevant aspects of the Pilgrim Players repertory, I have chosen to concentrate upon three of their productions that played regularly in their repertory. Each in its own way reflected the way in which Martin Browne sought to produce plays which, to one degree or another, fulfilled his concept of religious drama.

In his introduction to *Religious Drama* [Radius/SPCK, 1959] Browne sought to define the meaning of that term:

"It is the drama of which the theme is the relationship between God and man." [55]

The following three plays each explore, with varying degrees of dramatic effectiveness and genre, that relationship 'between God and man.'

Tobias and the Angel **by James Bridie**

This play had been written by Bridie in the same year (1930) as the play which was to establish his reputation as a playwright, *The Anatomist*. James Bridie [1888–1951] was the pseudonym of Osborne Henry Mayor. In addition to his reputation as a playwright, Bridie is also remembered for his crucial role in the founding of both the Glasgow Citizen's Theatre and the first College of Drama in Scotland in 1950.

The play under discussion was one of a number of biblical dramas that Bridie wrote and may best be considered as a light-hearted dramatic parable. Based on a traditional story from the Jewish Apocrypha, it tells the story of Tobias and his family. At the outset of the play they are experiencing difficulties that are the consequence of the father's past, unrepaid charity towards others. However, the old man's charity and practical expression of his simple faith are recognised, and the Archangel Raphael appears in the guise of a servant to lead Tobias on a path of growing maturity and self-knowledge. This itself eventually results in a happy and just resolution for all. Stated in these terms, the plot and characters seem well designed only for cliché and melodrama. The play is saved from the worst excesses of both through the rounded naturalism of the characters and the characteristic quality of Bridie's work: a dry wit and irony that infuses the dialogue at its

---

55. E Martin Browne, *Introduction to Religious Drama* (Radius/SPCK, 1959), p.ix.

best moments. For example, note here Bridie's gentle satire of official bureaucratic indolence through the character of Tobit's wife Anna, who works as a cleaner in Old Testament Assyria:

> I was working in the Government offices today. It is a pleasant rest to work in the Government offices. It is their reposeful atmosphere that is so soothing. [56]

In a later scene in the play, Tobit is talking to his future wife and Bridie delightfully employs contemporary colloquial references to the popular culture of his native Scotland, whilst simultaneously casting a glancing blow at the then current, and urgent, need for social welfare and reform:

> Sarah: They tell me that Nineveh is very beautiful. We have a song about the Bonnie, Bonnie Banks of the Tigris.
> Tobias: No. It's not very beautiful ... And we have some dreadful slums.
> Sarah: How horrid! Are you interested in social welfare?
> Tobias: No. Not much. My father is. He does quite a lot. [57]

It is that skilful use of dramatic irony and the interweaving of anachronistic references with naturalistic conventions that gives the play its interest and edge. This technique and approach are also an interesting means of communicating well-worn moral considerations, in a way that is entertaining without being piously didactic. It is not difficult to see why the play enjoyed such popular success within the company's repertory. If this play is an example of a writer adopting the appropriate style and register and, in the process, acknowledging its limitations; then in my judgment the next play to be considered is an example of entirely the opposite.

David by D H Lawrence

I mentioned earlier in this chapter how this play had provided Martin Browne with his first professional acting role with the Stage Society. It was perhaps partly this earlier acquaintance with the play, and its clear biblical subject matter, that drew him to it. However, I have to say that I find the play totally unsatisfactory in style and dramatic effect. Unlike Lawrence's better known *A Collier's Friday Night*, where there is that typically powerful, psychological insight into the lives of those Nottinghamshire mining families amongst whom Lawrence himself grew up, the historical and cultural distancing of *David* seems to have presented insurmountable difficulties to him. Based firmly on the biblical account of the ascendancy of the boy David over the decline of the insane Saul, Lawrence has chosen a style of dramatic language which seeks to emulate that of the Authorised Version of the Bible, whilst lacking any of that translation's poetry.

---

56. James Bridie, *Tobias and the Angel* (London, Constable, 1956), Act 2, p.9.
57. Ibid, p.39.

Although he adopts a naturalistic setting and characterisation, the characters frequently lapse into a rhetorical and declamatory style, which is both embarassingly melodramatic in its effect whilst conspiring to make the characters one-dimensional:

> David: [alone] Now, if Jonathan comes not, I am lost. This is the fourth day and evening is nigh. Lo! Saul seeketh my life ... Yea, Michael, thou art not far from me. Yet art thou distant even as death. I hide and have hidden. Three days have I hidden, and eaten scant bread. Lo! Is this to be the Lord's anointed! Saul will kill me and I shall die! [58]

There are, in addition, moments of unintended humour, when Lawrence seems, almost unwittingly, to place colloquialisms into the midst of the otherwise self-consciously mannered dialogue:

> David: But yet, O King, thy servant has heard it is a hard thing to be a witch, a work of silent labour and of years. And this maiden your daughter is not silent, I think, nor does she seem to waste her young brows in secret labours.
> Jonathan: That is true enough. She is a feather-brain. [59]

These weaknesses within the play are evidence of a failure to adopt the appropriate style of dramatic language for the subject matter, a confusion of genres. Whilst in this instance Lawrence fails conclusively, especially in relation to the outstanding achievements of his major literary output, it is a problem that is perhaps less particular to Lawrence in this case. Rather, it raises the wider issue of whether or not there is a satisfactory dramatic language for what is, in effect, a tragic theme framed within a religious context. It is not appropriate or possible, within the context of this chapter or book, to deal with this major critical issue. It has been examined most thoroughly in George Steiner's *The Death of Tragedy*.

In the following extract, Steiner argues that the convention of the verse tragedy no longer has currency for contemporary theatre and society:

> Ibsen and Chekhov ... had shown that prose and the economy of realism – the daylit, secular furnishings of common experience – could provide theatrical conventions relevant to the modern world, yet as rich and persuasive as those of verse tragedy. The verse tragedies produced by modern European and American poets are exercises in archaeology and attempts to blow fire into cold ash. It cannot be done ... the realism of Ibsen and Chekhov is a discipline of unfolding insight whose authority leads from the real of the letter to the more real of the spirit. The walls of the drawing room in an Ibsen play are transparent to the radiance or blackness of the controlling vision. [60]

---

58. D H Lawrence, *David*, in *Religious Drama/1*, selected and introduced by Marvin Halverson, (New York, Meridian Books, 1959), p.264.
59. Ibid, p.189.
60. George Steiner, *The Death of Tragedy* (Faber, 1974), pp. 303–5.

Professor Una Ellis-Fermor also questions, albeit from a very different critical perspective, the extent to which religious drama can successfully explore and deal with the diverse range of human experience as opposed to merely illustrating ethical or doctrinal views:

> There are several hundred plays of this kind, but how often do we find a play in which the fire and illumination that is the essence of religious experience become the central forms, as Macbeth's ambition, Othello's jealousy, Clytemnestra's hatred becomes the central force of their plays? [61]

The final play under consideration represents the liturgical form of religious drama referred to by Ellis-Fermor. It is a twentieth-century play employing the liturgical structure and genre of the earliest medieval drama.

The Way of the Cross by Henri Ghéon.

Henri Ghéon [1875–1943] like his countryman and contemporary playwright André Obey [1892–1975] was an important figure in the revival of twentieth-century verse drama. Also, both writers were attracted to religious/philosophical themes and concerns and had their plays premiered by Jacques Copeau and his Vieux-Colombier theatre company, itself a notable experiment in seeking to combine theatre practice with a community lifestyle. Through the work of his nephew, Michel Saint-Denis, Copeau's style was to have a profound impact upon modern British theatre, through his later work with George Devine at their Theatre Studio.

In the antiphonal nature and structure of the poetic verse employed by Ghéon and also the use of a Chorus from whom individuals in the narrative emerge and then return, this play clearly represents the dramatic form that Steiner asserts no longer has cultural or ideological currency. Nevertheless, in its evocation of the Passion and Resurrection of Christ, based on the Catholic Stations of the Cross, I feel it comes closest to reflecting and expressing Martin Browne's self-acknowledged orientation. In performance, this sense of the theatrical sign visibly signifying the 'Otherness' of a transcendent reality, invisible, is suggested in the following observation made by Henzie Browne to the play in performance: "They [i.e. the Chorus] are spectators who are, as it were, outside time and space, who suddenly change into a tragic embodiment of the things they see." [62]

In April 1943, changes in both the administration of the company and also its acting personnel, made the need for new plays urgent and Browne once again contacted his friend Eliot. The following is an extract from a letter from Browne to Eliot at this time:

---

61. Una Ellis-Fermor, *The Frontiers of Drama* (Methuen, 1945), p.4.
62. Henzie Browne, p.123.

I was inclined to ask you to discuss with me the acceptance of a commission for a play. Length, an hour or longer. Treatment suitable for production without a front curtain or a realistic setting, and in church if desired ... Cast not above ten and preferably smaller: It is not advisable to make more than half of it male, if you want the best quality of performance, at present ... I do not feel that it need be a conventionally religious subject, even for church, since if you write it, it will be a Christian play. [63]

Through this extract, one gains further confirmation of the limited conditions in which the company generally performed, with little or no opportunity for 'front curtain or a realistic setting'. Furthermore, Browne's reference to the size and and composition of the cast for the proposed play, implies the difficulty of finding male actors of sufficient quality and experience. Also of interest, of course, is his reference to the implicitly religious nature of Eliot's writing. In Browne's admission that a play need not necessarily have explicit religious theme to be a 'religious play' it suggests a more open-minded perspective on this issue than has sometimes been assumed. Nevertheless, it was allegedly the orthodoxy of Browne's religious thinking and definition of religious drama that led to Richard Ward and Phoebe Waterfield leaving the Pilgrim Players in the early months of its existence.

Whilst a fuller description of Ward's views are more appropriately discussed in the following chapter, I think that it's useful at this point to give an example of Ward's more liberal and radical thinking regarding religious belief and practice. The following quotation comes from an article published in the June 1940 issue of *The Adelphi* and is entitled 'A Tribunal Statement'. Although this article is not accompanied by Ward's name, Bill Hetherington, archivist of the PPU, who made this document available to me, believes that all circumstantial evidence points almost certainly to Ward being its author. I have carefully examined the article, compared its content and style vith other articles by Ward, and concur with Hetherington. In the article, the author states that:

Religion for me is not so much a matter of belief in dogma, or of being a member of an organised Church, as of inward mystical experience. That inward ... experience has revealed to me that it is a duty of human beings to foster the seed of divinity which is in every man, and that the meaning of Christianity is the unity of man in the love that is God. [64]

The emphasis upon experience and inner communion, rather than formal belief in a prescribed dogma, is characteristic of both the Quaker tradition and also in some Eastern religions, particularly Buddhism. Such sentiments are also expressed in Ward's earlier articles from *Peace News* discussed in my

---

63. Martin Browne, *T S Eliot's Plays*, p.160.
64. R H Ward (attributed), 'A Tribunal Statement', *The Adelphi*, 16, no 9, June 1940.

previous chapter. What is also very significant is that the 1940 article represents a 'Tribunal Statement' and we may clearly infer, therefore, that the sentiments expressed in it correspond to the moral basis offered by Ward his own conscientious objection.

For Martin Browne, his own more formal religious understanding necessarily determined and permeated much of his work with the Pilgrim Players. It should be remembered however that, like Ward with his own Adelphi company, the company members did not all subscribe to a commonality of belief. Browne's defining of the relatively egalitarian structure of the Pilgrim Players, based on the ethical communism of the early church, and his choice of plays for repertory, signal the relationship between his own beliefs and the structure and repertory of the Pilgrim Players. When Richard Ward therefore criticised Browne and his company for not being a 'revolutionary movement in the theatre' and for 'endeavouring to rehabilitate the old', one has to assess these comments in the broader context of Ward's own thinking regarding both theatre and its relationship to society.

In concluding this chapter, I want firstly to briefly outline the effective winding-down of the Pilgrim Players, certainly as a touring company, from the summer of 1943. For various personal reasons, including individual company members getting married, and the Brownes arranging for the return of their sons from America, where they had been sent for safety at the time of the Blitz, the company temporarily disbanded during May 1943. A different administrative and financial arrangement was made with CEMA and in the autumn of that year, some of the former company members rejoined Browne to establish the Pilgrim Players on its new basis. In 1945, at the immediate cessation of the war in Europe, Martin Browne leased the Mercury Theatre from Ashley Dukes to produce a season of new religious plays under the Pilgrim Players management and funded by CEMA. It was originally envisaged that, following on their conventional repertory at the Mercury, they would tour venues nationally. This project was launched in September 1945 and there was early critical and commercial success with Ronald Duncan's *This Way to the Tomb*. This success enabled Browne to run two other new verse dramas in repertory with the Duncan play: *The Old Man of the Mountains* by Norman Nicholson and *The Shadow Factory* by Ann Ridler. Martin Browne also commissioned *A Phoenix Too Frequent* from Christopher Fry, and in doing so gave the author his first London production. Unfortunately, from the viewpoint of this early success, Dukes returned from his post with the Allied Central Commission in Germany in 1948 and, rather acrimoniously, gave the company notice to quit.

These strained circumstances abruptly ended what had looked to be a successful experiment In the repertory of new plays. The Pilgrim Players therefore came to a close in 1948, although Pamela Keily continued to tour with her New Pilgrim Players.

Martin Browne went on to enjoy further success and wider critical acclaim with his productions of Eliot's *The Cocktail Party* [1949], *The Confidential Clerk*

[1953] and *The Elder Statesman* [1958]. In addition to reviving the performance of the York Cycle of Mystery Plays in 1951, he became head of the British Drama League from 1948 to 1957. He and his wife also worked regularly as visiting lecturers – with Martin Browne being awarded a Professorship – in Religious Drama at the Union Theological Seminary in New York. He was also President of RADIUS.

I should next like to offer two complementary views of the Pilgrim Players: one, derived from an anecdotal, primary source, first-hand account, and the second from a secondary critical source. Together, they help to offer an assessment of the achievements of the Pilgrim Players that combines the personal/subjective with the critical/objective. Nina Evans, a former actress with the company whom I interviewed in 1987, recalled that:

> The most enduring quality and aspect of that time was the sense of community that we shared ... I have never experienced anything quite like it since, and in a sense, neither do I expect to. [65]

Whilst George Rowell observes that:

> It is salutary to reflect that while the repertory movement owes its survival and standard, at least from the 1950's, to increasingly generous support (via the Arts Council) and local (from the ratepayer's pockets) assistance, that assistance was first conceived as helping to bring music and drama to threatened deprived areas by way of the touring unit.
>
> The precedent was set by purely private initiatives, grants from the Pilgrim Trust (founded by the Harkness family, an American philanthropic venture) and Carnegie Foundation to certain artistic endeavours. Notable amongst these was the work of the Pilgrim Players under Martin Browne, whose tour of the beleaguered south coast in the summer of 1940 with *Murder in the Cathedral* and *Tobias and the Angel* was a gesture of faith in the country and in its artistic values. [66]

65. Nina Evans, in interview with the author, Hampstead, August 1987.
66. Rowell and Jackson, pp.76–7.

3

THE ADELPHI PLAYERS
AND ADELPHI GUILD THEATRE

The Adelphi Players were founded by R H [Richard] Ward early in 1941 following hard on the heels of the publication of his article 'Theatre of Persons' in *The Adelphi* magazine. The company's initial base was a country house called The Oaks at Langham near Colchester in Essex. First rehearsals began there on 12 May 1941. The late John Headley, one of the early company members, recalls:

> We were not the first company of this kind ... at the beginning of the war the Pilgrim Players had been set up by Martin Browne to specifically tour around religious drama, which they interpreted in a fairly narrow way. We used to meet them up at intervals on the road. Richard Ward ... was very keen to start his own company on slightly different lines. We started off in a very simple way, just eight of us; I think that there were five men and three women. We started with *The Little Plays of St Francis* [Housman] and we started off in the summer of 1941, touring around Essex by road, carrying our simple props. by hand and travelling by bus and train to the villages and churches in Essex. In the beginning Richard got a grant of £50 from the SPCK [Society for the Propagation of Christian Knowledge] and this financed our first rehearsal period. After that we were effectively self-supporting. [1]

The Oaks was at this time a self-supporting pacifist/socialist community which I shall discuss in more detail shortly. Max Plowman, who ran the Centre and also edited *The Adelphi* magazine, was a close friend and mentor to Ward and a supporter of the fledgling company. Ward and Plowman had enjoyed a close friendship which dated back to 1936 when they had met through their mutual involvement in the PPU. Plowman had served during the First World War but, along with contemporaries such as Sassoon, Owen and Graves, came to criticise the conflict for its appalling and unjustifiable loss of lives. Plowman is remembered as both a leading and distinguished authority on William Blake, in addition to his writings on Pacifism. One famous example of this genre was his authorship of the pamphlet *The Right to Live* which was published in 1918. *The Adelphi* was a literary magazine that had been started in 1923 as a monthly literary journal under the editorship of John Middleton Murry, intended as a platform in particular for the writings of D H Lawrence. From 1927 it became a quarterly entitled *The New Adelphi*.

---

1. John Headley, recorded interview with author, April 1990.

Murry's editorship ended in this period with a Lawrence memorial in 1930 and the periodical became *The Adelphi*, incorporating *The New Adelphi*, which ran until 1955. Contributors during that twenty-five year period included Yeats, Eliot, Wells, Day-Lewis, Orwell, Ward and Auden. For Auden, the publication of some of his verse in the magazine in the early nineteen thirties represented the first occasion that his poetry was published in a literary journal with a national reputation and readership. The following extract offers an insightful recollection of both the magazine and also of the broader ideological ethos in which it was contextualised. The author is Clifford Williams who was a conscientious objector at the outbreak of war in 1939:

> One thread I must pick up and trace back to my early socialist days – the thread represented by *The Adelphi*, a magazine founded in 1923 by John Middleton Murry ... transformed by the time I encountered it ten years later into a literary monthly loosely affiliated to the Independent Labour Party. Murry's inner wrestlings with Marx and Blake ... had brought him, through the great-hearted Max Plowman, to pacifism ...
>
> *The Adelphi* became the literary platform for pacifists, standing in relation to the Peace Pledge Union as it had previously done to the Independent Labour Party. The ILP, or what remained of it by 1938, was anti-war on strictly ideological grounds; but Max Plowman's pacifism, and hence Murry's, was not primarily political but ethical and spiritual, like Blake's or, for that matter, George Fox's. Max Plowman actually became, for a time, General Secretary of the PPU. [2]

Before proceeding on to my specific discussion and examination of The Adelphi Players and, later, the The Adelphi Guild Theatre, I want to consider in more detail The Oaks, or, as it was otherwise known, The Adelphi Centre. Not only did the Centre and the journal provide Ward's theatre company with a name, but also with a broader ideological background of values and expectations.

The Necessity of Pacifism: Middleton Murry and The Adelphi Centre

In 1937, John Middleton Murry's book *The Necessity of Pacifism* was published, following on from his earlier *The Necessity of Communism*. In his 1937 book, from which the following is an extract, he discusses the development of his own political and ethical thinking which led to his founding of The Adelphi Centre:

> Capitalism was much more than an economic system: it was a social morality, an all-pervading spiritual atmosphere – nothing less, indeed, than a total 'life-mode'. Unless Socialists were prepared to challenge, first of all in themselves, the blind

---

2.   Clifford Williams, [ed] *The Objectors* (Gibbs and Phillips, 1965), p.91.

conformity to this 'life-mode'; unless they had imagination enough to realize the strength and subtlety of the thing they had to overthrow, they would merely be fighting the economics of Capitalism with the ethics of Capitalism: and they were bound to lose ... The Adelphi Centre is a centre for Socialists, founded by Socialists and conducted by Socialists. The Socialist movement, as understood by the founders of the Adelphi Centre, is based on the conviction of the desirability of a classless Society ... Some Socialists believe that it can be reached only through violent revolution; others that it can be attained by the peaceful methods of political democracy; yet others hold that a change in the hearts and minds of men is necessary; and all three may believe that 'the emancipation of the working-class must be the work of the working-class itself'. [3]

Murry intended that the Adelphi Centre should be non-sectarian and welcomed Socialists who were sympathetic to its basic ethos. The central aim of the community was to provide social and economic material conditions and an ideological climate in which Socialism could be realistically and practically applied. Murry also believed that through the dynamics of community life, the inner transformation that he believed was essential for the ultimate realisation of Socialism and the overthrowing of Capitalism, might at last be achieved. He envisaged that the community living at the Centre would revolve around a relatively permanent nucleus of twelve people, half of whom would be middle-class with some form of economic [job] security, and the other half working-class unemployed. In addition to this nucleus would be groups and individuals who would visit the Centre for varying degrees of time and contribute to its life. Murry believed that the Centre, as an example of embryonic Socialist community living, might be part of a wider movement offering an alternative to the emerging Fascist ascendancy across Europe:

> Today one can easily conceive of society so chaotic and barbarous that a Socialist movement which had educated itself into community and frugality would be the sole indigenous vehicle of the continuity of civilisation. [4]

There is a reference to the Adelphi Centre in the published diaries of Frances Partridge, *A Pacifist's War*:

> [Diary Date: 13 February 1941] A discussion about what work is consistent with pacifist views – canteens for instance, either for the military or otherwise ... How much one should voice one's views was the next question ... Max Plowman and Middleton Murry are trying to form a community on the Bruderhof plan. [5]

---

3. John Middleton Murry, *The Necessity of Pacifism* (Jonathan Cape, 1937), pp.79–81.
4. Ibid, p.88.
5. Frances Partridge, *A Pacifist's War* (Robin Clark, 1983), p.80.

Frances Partridge and her husband, Robin, were both Pacifists and had been associated with the Bloomsbury Group. It is interesting to note her reference to the 'Bruderhof' who were a community of Christian Pacifists, committed to a life of material simplicity and egalitarianism.

Depending on one's own perspective, it is perhaps easy to be critical of Middleton Murry's initiative. Certainly, the crude social engineering involved provides grounds for serious reflection as to whether the Adelphi Centre could ever have constituted a legitimate or lasting basis for the realisation of Socialist principles. Also in the context of the grimly inevitable rise of Fascism on the continent, his assertion that a community like The Oaks might act as a prototype of alternative resistance is naively optimistic.

Nevertheless, whilst the The Oaks may not have achieved the long-term aims of Murry and others involved, it fulfilled a significant role in providing a location where a diverse cross-section of Socialists could meet and share ideas. Furthermore, it also housed fifty Basque children – refugees of the Spanish Civil War – during the time of that conflict. Ward had already had a disillusioning experience of community life with the Abbey Gardens Community, run along similar lines to The Oaks. Plowman recognised that the younger Ward's energies could be better used in his commitment to tour with his own theatre company, and readily supported its formation. Much to Ward's profound sorrow, during the first few weeks of rehearsals, Plowman died. Middleton Murry resumed editorship of the magazine and continued to extend help to the seminal company. However, Ward's commitment to the Centre effectively waned with the death of his close personal friend and mentor, Max Plowman. With the vast majority of London's theatres closed during the early period of the war and with the suffering endured by its citizens, Ward decided that The Adelphi Players should start performing there late in 1941. Before continuing on to my examination of The Adelphi Players, it is important to give further consideration to Ward's wider thinking, especially Theatre of Persons, his manifesto article on theatre and society.

R H Ward and the Theatre of Persons

In order to examine what Ward meant by this concept, I shall quote from the article of the same name that appeared in the January 1941 edition of *The Adelphi*:

> It [The Theatre of Persons] is a theatre which offers its audiences experience, the experience first and foremost of seeing themselves face to face. The real function of the theatre is one of illumination, the casting of light upon the familiar, so that it can be seen fully and for what it is. And the familiar, where the common man is concerned, is the whole range of his inward and outward life, his thoughts and sensations and actions. The theatre, by presenting them within the vision and the wholeness which belong to art and the artist, can make them intelligible. It can so

illuminate them that someone watching them happening on the stage to persons like himself may understand them objectively in a way he can never do when he himself is the protagonist and knows them only subjectively. [6]

Theatre is here defined as a catalyst for stimulating the awareness and raising the consciousness of the audience. This is not, of course, in the agit-prop sense of a politicised understanding leading to direct political action and activity. As I made clear in my opening chapter, Ward felt that whatever usefulness such theatre might have had prior to the war was now redundant. Rather, in Ward's thinking, there is an intrinsic sense of theatre operating on an existential level or almost in terms of a psychodrama in which theatre facilitates deeper insights and understandings. There are clearly echoes of Aristotle's concept of catharsis and, to a lesser extent, Stanislavski's concept of the illuminating, empathetic, insightful relationship that he insisted should exist between actor and audience. Later on in the same article Ward goes on to discuss and define theatre in terms of allegory, and draws parallels with the function of theatre as a means of opening human consciousness. This process is signalled through the iconic characters from the classic plays of the western european tradition:

> For the theatre is an allegory, and must be so treated by those who work in it. It puts into new words and new dresses things that we all know, and by its vividness ... brings to the human mind, even by shock methods, comprehension of things so ordinary, so deeply rooted in nature and history, that we pass them by as too familiar. As the life of Christ is an allegory of what all human life may be and much human life consciously is, so the great plays *Faust*, *Hamlet* and *Oedipus* – are the stories of ourselves, revealing us for our own understanding. It is in terms of allegory that the theatre must be understood. [7]

There are several issues which I wish to address from this extract. Ward's concept of theatre as 'allegorical' is clearly based on two assumptions. These can be expressed as an assumption regarding human consciousness and another concerned with the nature and function of theatre in itself. There is a view of a common and universal consciousness which constitutes a form of narrative: 'the stories of ourselves'. Furthermore, and here lies Ward's second assumption, that meta-narrative of human existence and consciousness may be facilitated, evoked and realised through 'the great plays' of a specifically western, european tradition and canon. In one important sense, I think that these assumptions within Ward's thinking reflect his strong and abiding interest in Jungian psychoanalysis. In this, he shared an enthusiasm and belief that characterised a considerable proportion of writers and artists on the broad left.

---

6.   R H Ward, 'Theatre of Persons', *The Adelphi*, (1941), 122–26, (p.122.)
7.   Ibid, p.124.

In another important sense, Ward's struggle to define what I might call a 'Theatre of Transcendence', has undeniable resonance with the attempts of Peter Brook, in 1968, to try to define a 'Holy Theatre': "I am calling it the Holy Theatre for short, but it could be called The Theatre of the Invisible-Made-Visible: the notion that the stage is a place where the invisible can appear has a deep hold on out thoughts." [8]

Against this notion of the theatre as a means of revealing transcendent truths and mysteries of human existence, one must propose a more sociological, cultural materialist view such as that argued by the Marxist theatre practitioner, John McGrath:

> You go into a space, and some other people use certain devices to tell you a story ... while you are there, they make a choice, with political implications, as to which story they tell – and how to tell it ... What does this mean then? That not all stories are so wonderfully universal? That the political and social values of the play cannot be the same for one audience as they are for another? ... what most of us do – we take the point of view of a normal person – usually that of a well-fed, white, middle-class, sensitive but sophisticated literary critic: and we universalise it as the response. [9]

Whilst there is clearly not the appropriate time or direct relevance to enter into this debate more fully within this chapter or this book, I do believe that it important to raise those issues arising from Ward's article. Ward's contribution to what is effectively a continuing debate about the relationship of theatre to society and politics of performance is, I think, interesting and stimulating.

Within his article, Ward goes on to make two further principal points. One is related to his analysis of the relationship between theatre and society and for a radical restructuring of both in the post-war period. The second deals with his interest in, and commitment to, the staging of Shakespeare: incorporating the progressive approaches of Poel and others.

Ward wastes no sympathy on what he sees as an 'irretrievably corrupt, commercial theatrical establishment':

> When a civilisation is shaken to its foundations, it is the more insecure portions ... which crumble first. The theatre has been insecure for a long time, a showy and garish facade, reared upon the shifting sands of fashion and money; and inwardly hollow, having no roots in the hidden but ... potent realities without which none of our institutions will stand in these days. Whatever emerges from this war (and the commercial theatre, the racket we have made believe was theatre, will not) must emerge transformed. There was something rotten in the status quo and that

8.   Peter Brook, *The Empty Space* (Pelican, 1969), p.47.
9.   John McGrath, *A Good Night Out* (Methuen, 1981), pp.1–3.

manifestation of the theatre's life is dead for good ... a new theatre will arise, founded once more upon those certainties of religion and the arts which the old dead theatre forsook. [10]

Ward's views are, once again, an interesting combination of radical, modernist, cultural analysis with a concept of theatre that is characterised by late nineteenth-century, Hegelian ethics and, in his concept of religion and the arts, Aristotelian concepts. Whilst Ward's analysis and hopes for a transformed, post-war theatre were not realised in the sense that he believed, this reflects in parts a failure to discern the wider financial power-base underlying the commercial theatrical establishment. This is an issue that I will discuss in more detail in my concluding chapter. Furthermore, it is fair to comment that the kind of radical idealism informing Ward's thinking was a common characteristic of much broad left thinking in this period, especially in the context of the ideology of the anti-Fascist front. Finally in relation to this issue for the moment, a 'new theatre' did arise, of course, in the post-war period following on the *annus mirabilis* of 1956. The wider and fuller implications of that social and cultural sea-change will be addressed in considerable detail in my final chapter. As far as Ward's thinking was concerned in relation to the production of Shakespeare, the following extract from 'Theatre of Persons' makes clear his commitment to Poel's experiments:

> Shakespeare's audiences, when told that they were looking at another part of the wood, believed it and were left free by a nearly naked stage to watch the play. Lately, it has not been possible to see the play for the trees; a good play needs no bushes, when a good play does speak for itself, it speaks the truth ... If the theatre is to speak directly of the realities of human life, to persons needing an understanding of those realities, it must be allowed, both by actors and producers, to say its say in terms of sincerity and simplicity. Such a theatre does not lose its magic. Nothing can take the magic of illusion from the theatre (even the cinema has not quite done that) for the theatre is illusion, just as church ritual is illusion. This illusion is the instrument by which human consciousness is opened to a fuller understanding of the realities that permeate and underlie nature. [11]

This extended extract from Ward's essay confirms, essentially, the principal theoretical aspects of his model of theatre. His assertion that theatre functions as an 'instrument' or catalyst for the heightening of human consciousness relates closely, I believe, to his strong interest in Jungian psychoanalysis. Tied in with this theoretical strand is a form of late or post-Romantic sentiment that the natural, material world is effectively a visible expression of 'the realities that permeate nature'. What emerges, I believe, from these constituent

---

10.　Ward, 'Theatre of Persons', p.122.
11.　Ibid, p.124.

elements is an ideological position that incorporates a modernist, proto-Marxist analysis of society and culture with an ethical, post-Romantic understanding of both Nature and human consciousness. Therefore, implicit within Ward's title of his essay is a liberal, egalitarian, humanist assertion of the centrality of human beings: "In a word, the theatre must be seen in terms of persons; the transformed theatre must be a theatre of human beings, run by human beings and for the sake of other human beings." [12]

When Ward argues for a 'theatre of human beings', he is surely advocating that same humanistic concern for the centrality and integrity of the individual that he discusses in his previously mentioned article 'The Human Factor' [*Peace News*, 1939]: "The world is what we make it, and when we refuse to be human beings, to be persons and treat others as persons, we make it hell."

    Whilst it is not possible or appropriate to enter into a detailed discussion of Hegelian ethics within the context of this book, it is important, nevertheless, to recognise its significance as a reference point for Ward's own thinking. Ninian Smart identifies a central tenet of Hegelian philosophy:

> What we take to be the material world [Hegel argued] is in fact the product of mind. But this would be a paradoxical and frivolous doctrine if it were taken to mean that the world is created by my mind. On the contrary, the world is the product of an Absolute Mind, distinct from individual minds, but containing them within itself. The stuff of reality, then, is spiritual rather than material. [13]

Within this wider Hegelian philosophical context, the ethical perspective inherent within Ward's thinking becomes even more clearly contextualised. At the risk of over-simplification, if all reality is the product of a metaphysical, metaphorical 'God' as 'Absolute Mind', and the material world is a visible expression of that underlying reality, then Ward's understanding of theatre as an instrument for 'revealing' that reality becomes more readily definable. There are undoubtedly contradictions inherent in a conceptual viewpoint that seeks to reconcile, as Ward's thinking did at this time, an ethical idealism with a more radical, materialist analysis of social, economic and political structures.

    In concluding this section on the nature and implications of Ward's thinking in relation to his theatre work, I wish to quote extensively from a letter written by Ward to John Crockett, dated 28 February 1941, just prior to the formation of The Adelphi Players. The letter has clear value as a first-hand, primary source document, and, in that, as a clear indicator of both Ward's thinking at this time and of the social conditions of bomb-ravaged London:

12. Ibid, p.122.
13. Ninian Smart, *The Religious Experience of Mankind* (Collins/Fontana, 1969), p.648.

Nothing much is happening here (though there was a shower of incendiaries in these parts, the nearest about twenty yards down the road, a night or so after I got back) [from visiting the Crocketts in Cornwall] but that only makes things worse. It's abject, it's passive and it's inhuman. I walked through a number of streets behind Victoria the other day and there it all was, the dreary abject vileness of it; street after street of damaged houses; boarded windows like closed eyes; the staircases in ruins, but the Woolworth shade still on the light fitting in the hall. There were the subhuman inhabitants of bombed London, shuffling out of their underground cellars and making for the Tube stations. Deep down in the earth is the only place where the only animal on two legs can feel secure. And yet, at the other extreme, we've discovered how to take ourselves miles up into the sky, but all we can do when we get there, God-like creatures that we are, is shit bombs onto the cities beneath ... I'd clear out now if I could; but I can't, either with a full pocket or a clear conscience. This seems to be the only place where we can earn our living at our proper jobs, and the more I see of it, the more I know I have got to get this theatrical company going and cart it around these ghastly deserts if it kills me. I will not give in to the whole vile situation and pretend that things like the theatre have got to shut down because there's a war on, or that it is too difficult to do such a job in these war conditions, or that nothing matters but the war, the war and again the war ... That's just what the swine want who're running this crazy circus, and keeping it running in their democracy and their non-existent 'freedom'. They can do what they bloody well like, but I'll go on trying to realise the things I stand for and they don't ... at least one has the satisfaction of knowing, even while the process starves you and blows your home to bits, that the thing's busting at last, busting to hell. But better crawl through hell in the hope of coming out the other side than carry on with the sort of thing that's been operating in these islands for the past two centuries. There is that much comfort in the war – that the bomb-dropping is nothing more than the shitting process of a decrepit and incontinent organism mortally scared ... Why don't more people of our generation understand what they're fighting for at the behest of the State, the Established Church and the Devil himself? (a fine unholy trinity) [14]

In considering this letter as an invaluable source of evidence of Ward's thinking just prior to his forming of The Adelphi Players, one necessarily recognises that, in a private letter written to a close friend sharing similar values, the degree of self-censorship is likely to be minimal. The passion of Ward's language and his denunciation of what he sees as the corrupt political establishment, which has resulted in war with all of its attendant sufferings, is clear and unequivocal. He also clearly views theatre as his means of making a 'proper living'. In two articles for *The Adelphi* of May and June 1940, Ward had, more formally and for a public readership, conveyed his anger concerning the war and its concomitant evils:

---

14. Richard Ward, in letter to John Crockett, dated 28 February 1941, loaned by kind permission of Wilfred Harrison, joint Literary Executor of Ward's estate.

I do not believe that a good world can be built by putting guns into the hands of those who will be called upon to build it. In war, the super-efficient machines of propaganda are employed in training people to lie, hate, distrust, defame; to bomb, burn, stab, and poison their similarly-trained fellows of another nation. I cannot believe that hate, lies, and suspicion are the bricks with which to build a just and benevolent world ... Today I look at the world about me, see liberties being taken from the people each day, see the people still the pawns of financial oligarchs ... [15]

With some old properties and costumes donated by a well-wisher, Richard Ward and the embryonic Adelphi Players left for London late in 1941. For about the first eight months they played exclusively there, in air raid shelters, bomb sites, church halls, public parks; indeed anywhere that they were called upon to perform. It is to that initial phase of Ward's practical commitment to touring theatre in wartime Britain that I now wish to turn.

The Adelphi Players: Company Structure and Organisation

The following review from *The Times* of an early production by The Adelphi Players is of interest:

The Adelphi Players have been doing splendid work in helping to keep the theatre alive in the adverse conditions of war; it is fitting that they should give their first performance of Housman's *Abraham and Isaac* at the Westminster Cathedral Hall, where their acting was sensitive and intelligent. [16]

The review confirms the fact that, by the end of summer 1941 – the date of the review – The Adelphis were already known and established in London. In terms of the location for the production, it also confirms the kind of non-standard venue that they usually found themselves in.

In *The Adelphi Players: The Theatre of Persons* by Cecil Davies, which I had the privilege of editing and providing an introduction for, there is a uniquely first-hand account and memoir of both The Adelphi Players and the later Adelphi Guild Theatre. In that account, Cecil Davies makes the following observation about the personnel of The Adelphi Players:

It would be absurd to suggest that the people Ward first gathered together were consciously filled with these ideas [Ward's theoretical aims]. They were very ordinary people, not all of whom had any real experience of theatre at all. [17]

---

15. R H Ward [attributed], 'A Tribunal Statement', *The Adelphi*, (1940), 369–71 (p.370).
16. 'Abraham and Isaac', *The Times*, 25 August 1941.
17. Cecil Davies, introduced and edited by Peter Billingham, *The Adelphi Players: The Theatre of Persons*, (Harwood Academic Publishers, 2001), p.9.

Another original member of the company, Greta Newell [later, Plowman] who had trained with Saint-Denis and Devine at their London Theatre Studio and had then worked in repertory theatre until the outbreak of war observed that:

> It's very interesting that every one of the women in the company had embarked as actresses whose careers had been interrupted by war because of the sort of theatre that Richard was offering. I don't think that any of the men had actually considered a theatrical career before. [18]

These 'very ordinary people' at the beginning included, along with Richard Ward and Phoebe Waterfield: Greta Newell, Jack Boyd Brent, Geoffrey Palmer and John Headley. Cecil Davies joined the company in its sixth week, transferring from his work – as a conscientious objector – as a baker's roundsman. Prior to that, he had achieved a First Class Honours degree in English at the University of London. He had also, unwittingly, been cynically used by the popular tabloid press – *The Daily Express* – as the subject of an article with only thinly-disguised, vituperative criticism of his position as a conscientious objector. The public animosity stirred up by the tone and intentions of the article forced him into hiding for his own safety for a short time. Such an incident indicates the potentially explosive tide of latent public prejudice towards conscientious objectors prior to the outbreak of war. [See Appendix B.] Jenny Ward, the founder's wife, was also an early company member, principally as costume designer and seamstress. Davies left the company temporarily in 1942 in the context of his marrying and receiving an invitation to join the Colchester Repertory Theatre. He was replaced by Wilfred Harrison under the circumstances referred to in my opening chapter.

Harrison went on, of course, to become a very close, life-long friend to Ward. Piers Plowman, son of the late Max, was also to join The Adelphi Players at a relatively early stage. However he ran into trouble with the authorities when he left his tribunal-approved work as a farm labourer to join them without official permission. For this display of unauthorised initiative he received a short prison sentence which he served. On his release, he went on to rejoin the company, becoming one of its best-liked members and a fine actor. He also, later, married Greta Newell. Bettina Headley [then, Stern] a cousin of John Crockett's wife, Anne, was also a regular member from 1942 onwards. John Headley describes how he first came into contact with Ward and the circumstances in which he was invited to join The Adelphi Players:

> I was working in an Educational Settlement in the Rhondda Valley before the war in a training scheme in joinery for disabled lads. We had a visit at the beginning of the war from the Old Vic, led by Sybil Thorndike and Lewis Casson,

---

18. Greta Plowman (née Newell), in recorded interview with author, April 1990.

and they did *The Medea* and *Macbeth*. I spent one afternoon taking Sybil around the Rhondda Valley visiting the Unemployed Clubs ... so I began to get interested in the theatre. So when Richard Ward came down with a Pilgrim production of *Tobias and the Angel* in our hall, someone had got 'flu and I had to stand in and got to know Richard. When he wanted to start his own company early in 1941, he persuaded me to come and join the company on the basis of organising transport, making props, and things like that. [19]

Like Ward himself, all of the male company members were conscientious objectors, though not all on the basis of Pacifist convictions. Their involvement with The Adelphi Players was recognised by the tribunals as 'War Work', the equivalent for many COs of land labour, ambulance work, etc.

However, there were many COs for whom even alternative work was seen as a contribution to the war effort and they refused to be allocated such tasks. For this they faced imprisonment whilst many others had their objections arbitrarily disallowed by tribunals. Remarkably, the Peace Pledge Union was able to continue to function and publish its *Peace News* throughout the war, despite constant harassment from the authorities and the shortage of paper for printing. Middleton Murry was the editor for most of the war years. It's worth quoting from one of the articles to appear from this period, to appreciate the unswerving and courageous ideological and ethical stance that the movement continued to take:

> At this time ... millions of human beings find themselves – simply because they have been born in one spot rather than another – flattered, bullied and conscripted by their respective fuehrers into two utterly artificial and hostile slave-societies, with their minds and bodies riveted to machines ... By freeing the human mind from the primal tribal obsessions which have made 20th-century man a cog in the great engines of war, pacifism has released him from the greatest tyranny and slavery of all. [20]

The combination of persons with diversely motivated anti-war convictions along with the unique venture of taking theatre to new venues and audiences understandably helped to define the progressive outlook of the company. In their insistence upon equal salaries for members and the central function of the regular participatory company meetings, The Adelphi Players – along with similar ventures such as The Pilgrim Players and the Mobile Units of the Unity Theatre – prefigured some of the small, but significant, developments that were to emerge through the theatre co-operatives of the later post-war period. Davies offers a recollection of those company meetings:

---

19. Headley,
20. Cited in Albert Beale, *Against All War: Fifty Years of Peace News 1936–86* (Peace News, 1986), p.14.

From the start, the chief instrument of organisation was the Company Meeting. This was attended by all members and in it anything connected with the life and work of the company could be discussed. At the first meeting at The Barn rehearsal room Langham, 1 May 1941, Ward described the proposed nature of the company. It was to have a co-operative basis; the privileges and responsibilities of members were to be equal; he himself was in a special position for the time as preliminary organiser and director. ... The small-part actor, stage manager, director – all accepted the same financial return for their work. In this way, the concept of the equal responsibility of members was translated into hard reality. [21]

Each company member received £2 per week when the company was in performance whilst there were equal billeting privileges, firstly at The Oaks and then, when The Adelphi Players began to tour more extensively, board and lodging would rely upon the hospitality of hosts at the various venues. For the first few weeks of its existence, The Adelphi Players received a subsidy of £10 a month from RADIUS. This was an informal arrangement and did not represent a commitment to long-term subsidy as such. Indeed, when this short term arrangement eventually ended, it was with some conviction that The Adelphi Players acknowledged that they were the only company of their kind who worked independently of any form of subsidy. The Adelphi Players were in fact 'subsidised' by two friends, one of whom lent the small van by which they made their early tours, whilst the other provided an interest-free loan of £50. In order to sustain this fragile financial basis, the company requested a minimum guarantee from most venues of about £5. By working on that basis, any small profits that did arise from their work was used to subsidise their performances in venues such as air raid shelters.

One cannot, of course, discuss matters of financial subsidy or otherwise without referring to CEMA whom I mention briefly in my previous chapter. CEMA – the Council for the Encouragement of Music and the Arts – was formed in April 1940 on a permanent basis 'to develop a greater knowledge, understanding and practice of the Fine Arts, to increase their accessibility to the public and to improve their standard of execution', as its stated aims declared. Under the harsh social and economic stringencies of wartime, it was clear that the promotion of the arts to the public could play a useful role and function as a morale-booster and propaganda exercise for the civilian population. In his book *Other Theatres* Andrew Davies refers to the fact that during this period expenditure on books doubled whilst educational bodies grew in membership numbers. The initial impetus for CEMA came from a private philanthropic source. Dr Thomas Jones administered an American-based charitable trust called the Pilgrim Trust. It was this Trust that provided the original funding for the setting up of the project, the Pilgrim Players being the first company to benefit from its funds. In his book *The Set Up*, Ronald Hayman names the original founding members of the Council as

---

21. Davies, pp.10–11.

'Dr Thomas Jones, Lord Macmillan [Minister of Information], Sir Walford Davies [a proponent of the People's Music Education initiative], Kenneth Clark and William Emrys Williams, who was Secretary of the British Institute of Adult Education and prior to the war had also instigated an 'Art for the People' scheme'. In April 1940 the financial basis for CEMA's work was that the Government would contribute, up to £50,000, a pound for every pound donated by private funding. However, this arrangement did not prove successful and by April 1942 the scheme had become entirely Government financed.

At this time, it also established Regional Offices with Panels that screened applications for funding from various groups and individuals. Lewis Casson was one of the travelling representatives of the Drama Panel and was responsible for funds being awarded to both the Pilgrim Players and – eventually – The Adelphi Players. I shall discuss the implications of the formation of CEMA and its eventual transformation into the Arts Council of Great Britain in my concluding chapter. CEMA's brief and function was naturally very similar to that provided by ENSA – the Entertainments National Service Association – which was established by Basil Dean and catered primarily for troops stationed overseas. Andrew Davies writes that 'In all, ENSA arranged 2 million shows during the war in front of a total audience estimated at over 300 million people'. [22] The role of CEMA necessarily involved the controlled provision of petrol for those companies engaged in touring professional theatre to the public. One might also argue that CEMA was also created, from a Government point of view, to monitor and oversee the work of companies such as The Adelphi Players who, in the light of the composition of its members, might be construed as representing a potential threat to the propaganda and ideology of the war effort. That they were never a 'Pacifist' or 'Political' theatre company was not necessarily a protection against Government interference. As I stated in my opening chapter, the Play Unit of the ABCA – staffed primarily by Socialist activists from the Unity Theatre – did come under intense scrutiny with Churchill endeavouring, unsuccessfully, to close the Unit down. Whilst The Adelphi Players were always conspicuously anti-propagandist and therefore did not pose a direct threat to the authorities, the centralised control of essential provisions such as petrol, and the monitoring of plays in performance, established the political machinery for ensuring that the situation remained as such. Returning to the practical details of the relationship between The Adelphi Players and CEMA, Cecil Davies recalls that:

> As the war situation became more acute, it became evident that some help might be needed in relation to the difficulties of wartime transport, including petrol, to personnel problems in relation to National Service and Entertainment Tax. The

22. Andrew Davies, *Other Theatres*. (Macmillan, 1987), p.130.

initial relationship of the company to CEMA was very friendly. In December 1942, Lewis Casson saw an Adelphi performance as a CEMA representative and, largely because of his support, an unconditional grant of £10 a month was made to the company pending further consideration. [23]

Lewis Casson and his wife, Sybil Thorndike, who herself was an active member of the PPU, were to be a constant source of support to the work of The Adelphi Players and, in fact, Casson was later to feature on one occasion as a Guest Director.

The Adelphi Players: Repertory

In the minutes of a company meeting dated 18 January 1942, Ward is quoted as follows regarding the issue of artistic policy for The Adelphi Players and the subsequent criteria for their repertory:

> The time is coming when our age must evolve, out of its own soul, its own theatre – and by theatre, I mean its own plays, its own methods of acting and presentation. So far as I can see, our day has no theatrical heart; the Old Vic is essentially a survival; the plays of Auden and Isherwood seem to have been abortive; the Unity has died of propaganda; it is just possible that – if I may say it – *Holy Family* [Ward's own verse drama] is a faint foreshadowing of what might be called the theatrical heart of the age. [24]

I have already discussed in my introduction the implications of Ward's analysis of the Old Vic, the plays of Auden and Isherwood and the Unity Theatre. Before proceeding to examine Ward's own play *Holy Family* and to discuss what Ward might have meant by 'the theatrical heart of the age', it is necessary to examine the three categories of plays that he felt the company should perform in repertory. He states these categories in the minutes from that same meeting:

> 1) Neo-Elizabethan, which he [Ward] explained as the revival of Elizabethan drama played under conditions and in a manner approximating to those which existed in Shakespeare's day, and also a contemporary drama written in similar form.
> 2) 'Odd Plays', by which he meant productions such as the current *Holy Family* which was a new departure in dramatic conception.
> 3) Intimate Plays, such as those written by Strindberg and certain other playwrights for performance to small audiences under conditions that brought them into more close and intimate contact with the actors than the usual large West End theatre afforded. [25]

---

23. Davies, correspondence.
24. Minutes of The Adelphi Players Company Meeting, dated 18 January 1942, loaned by kind permission of Cecil Davies.
25. Ibid.

In order to consider these categories in more detail, I shall examine three plays in repertory from this early period of The Adelphi Players' work. Each play represents one of the three categories defined by Ward.

1 Neo-Elizabethan

Dr Faustus by Christopher Marlowe. This production opened at The Adelphi Centre, Langham on 4 June 1941 and was withdrawn at Tunstall on 12 November 1942 after 108 performances.

In his *Adelphi* article of May 1940 'The Hope of Liberation', Ward had stated that 'Faust is the type of Western man, and his hell generated in himself and finally manifested in his outward world, is of his own making'.

It is perhaps not surprising therefore that he selected Marlowe's treatment of this fictive allegorical character as the first production under this category. Faust is also mentioned, of course, as one of the great plays by Ward in his 'Theatre of Persons' article. Dealing as it does with the pursuit of power and knowledge through the marrying of the will to occult, destructive forces, it must have carried an apocalyptic significance in the context of a corrupt Capitalist world order and the ascendancy of Hitler and his Nazi ideology of racial supremacy and global domination. Owing to the length of the 1604 Quarto and the size of the cast, Ward felt obliged to make considerable cuts. In terms of production style it appears to have embodied what Ward stated in relation to his views on the production of Shakespeare:

> Our job will be to present, not ourselves in fine clothes and mouthing fine speeches, but the play – the play on a naked stage, with a minimum of trimmings and properties, with all its amazing humanity and insight, all its vision of heaven and hell, all its poetry and humour and morality laid bare. Our job is to reveal the play, to be its servants. [26]

Three reviews of the play offer contrasting and interesting responses to the production:

> Their abridgements are open to question. All but one of the scenes in which Faustus has a chance to enjoy himself are cut, leaving only the scenes in which he bemoans his folly in selling his soul ... so that we obtain a one-sided picture. [27]

Whilst another critic observed that:

> Their shortened version preserves all the ethical points made by the play. [28]

And finally:

---

26. Ibid.
27. *The Letchworth Citizen*, 7 November 1941.
28. *The Birmingham Post*, 31 March 1942.

It is a vivid, arresting performance in which the true essence of the drama was achieved. The stage settings were of the simplest, serving to heighten the effectiveness of the players' accomplished art. [29]

There is a methodological issue that I wish to raise here, one which I alluded to in my opening chapter when discussing and defining my broader methodological approach in this book. I have been most fortunate in gaining access to a considerable amount of primary, first-hand, documentary evidence in relation to The Adelphi Players in particular. This evidence includes many newspaper reviews of the company in performance. The problem of how to evaluate these reviews as a source of evidence and reconstruction is a complex matter. Clearly, the principal value of such reviews is their first-hand, eye-witness nature. They offer the researcher and reader a unique glimpse of the plays and company in performance. Equally, the overriding, problematic issue is that of the inescapable subjectivity of the reviewer. This also introduces associated issues of the nature of the journal in which the review features and the accompanying audience for that journal. Of course, this matter is not one that is exclusive to this book. It has implications for all similar attempts to reconstruct, discuss and evaluate theatre in performance. In this particular context, the transient and transformed conditions of wartime Britain and its social and cultural life contribute to this sense of the indeterminance of both the cultural production and its reception. What I have endeavoured to do throughout is to try, where possible, to discover and offer viewpoints that represent a range of responses. Also, where visual evidence is also available, I have sought to provide it as an additional, corroborating evidence of the work in performance.

In respect to the production of *Dr Faustus*, I am able to offer visual evidence of the play in open-air production in the grounds of Worcester Cathedral. The date of this performance, directed by Ward, was 12 July 1942 and also shows him in the role of Faustus [right of photograph on page 72]. The other character seen in this photograph is Mephistopheles, played by Stanley Messenger. The setting is as simple – by necessity – as Ward had wished with a simple trestle stage, in a performance played effectively straight on to a good-sized audience.

Another revealing piece of evidence that I wish to offer in relation to this particular production is the following recollection offered by Cecil Davies in 1998 as a Retrospect for my edited treatment of his own account of the company. I believe that it offers a poignant and vivid insight into both the material circumstances of performance and also the ideological tenor of the company's work:

Christmas Day 1941 is never to be forgotten and has always seemed to me to epitomise our life and work. About midday we arrived with our very minimal

---

29. *The Nottingham Journal*, 17 April 1942.

The Adelphi Players in their production of Richard Ward's abridged version of Marlowe's *Dr Faustus*. Directed by Richard Ward. This photograph is of an open-air performance at Worcester Cathedral, 12 July 1942. The photograph shows Richard Ward (right) in the role of Faustus. Photograher: Unknown.

equipment at the United Services Club, almost in the shadow of Big Ben. We were made welcome and I recall that we had the use of the bar. Our performance was of Christopher Marlowe's *Tragical History of Dr Faustus* ... In that place and at that time, the hellish fall of Faustus, as a warning to mankind not 'To practise more than heavenly power permits' seemed to us to speak to the condition of a world at war. Our performance, as conscientious objectors, of Marlowe's tragedy in what we felt to be the very heart of militarism, would alone have been a noteworthy experience ... In the evening we went to Bethnal Green, where a huge tube-station, not yet in service for its proper function, acted as one of London's largest air raid shelters ... To our surprise we found that, unlike some shelters in which we had performed, this had been fully adapted for its purpose. Where the station was at its widest much of its width had been taken up by an auditorium and a stage with tabs and battens of lights. Here our play was Richard Ward's *Holy Family*, in its first version – the refreshingly heretical one – for which we wore modern dress, with no settings or properties save a three-legged stool for the pregnant Mary ... No doubt we were naive. It was only 1941. The worst of the war and the Holocaust were still to come, but it was Christmas Day and we had taken Marlowe's grim warning to the Forces and Richard Ward's vision of hope even in despair to the civilians of the underground. [30]

2   Odd Plays

Holy Family by Richard Ward. The second, revised production of this play opened at The Playhouse, Ilkley on 23 November 1942 and was withdrawn on 24 April 1943, at the Civic Playhouse, Bradford, after a total of 79 performances.

In the programme notes for this production Richard Ward stated:

> *Holy Family* is, frankly, experimental in form, an attempt to find dramatic expression for the thoughts and feelings of contemporary men and women and to make the Birth of Christ a present reality for ordinary people. [31]

It was with this play that Ward sought to try and define the kind of play that might point towards the transformed theatre of the age and one which he anticipated emerging after the defeat of Fascism and the ending of the war. In style it is an example of the religious verse drama genre discussed at some length in previous chapters. It incorporates an interesting stylistic device in having a Chorus who emerge from the body of the cast, appearing in various roles within the narrative of the play. The narrative of the Nativity myth is transposed into a contemporary setting with the characters representing ordinary people of that contemporary period. Davies refers to the 'refreshingly heretical' first version of this play. That original production had

---

30. Davies, pp.64–5.
31. R H Ward, Programme Note to *Holy Family*.

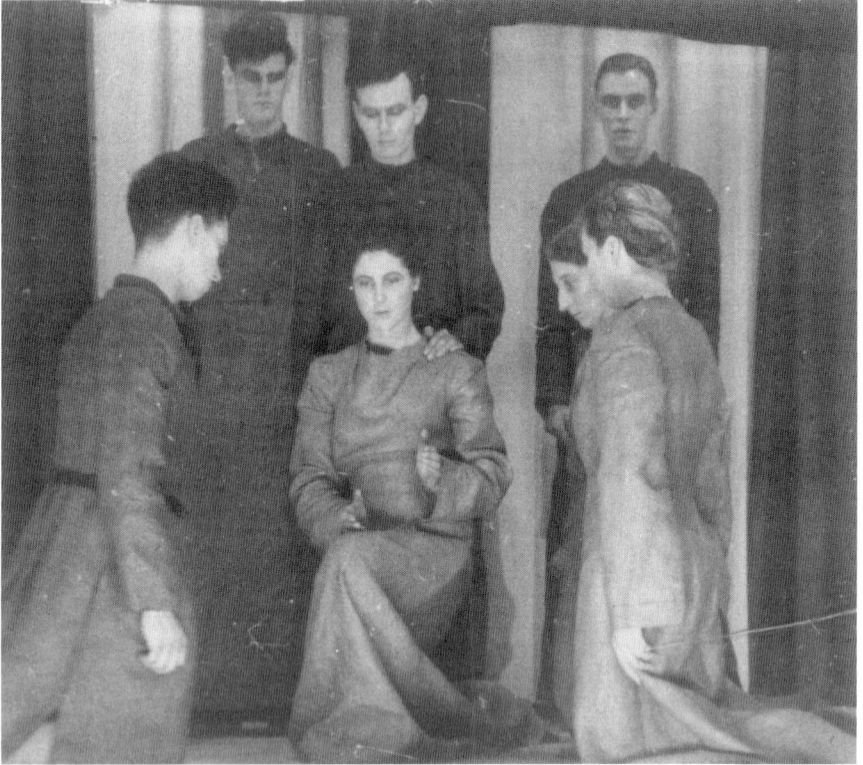

Richard Ward's *Holy Family*, Ilkley Playhouse, April 1942. Directed by Richard Ward. Featuring, left to right (standing), Wilfred Harrison, John Headley and Jack Boyd Brent; left to right (kneeling), Piers Plowman, Greta Newell, Phoebe Waterfield and Jane Fitzgerald. Photographer: Unknown.

attracted controversy in some religious quarters because it reflected Ward's, for that period, radical theological views. These were expressed most particularly in the depiction of the child Jesus as an ordinary human child, stressing the parenthood of Mary and Joseph. Following on from earlier expositions of his theological beliefs, the play depicts the child as an embodiment of human potential towards a radical kind of divinity as liberation and awareness, rather than the literal Incarnation of God. The play also serves as a critique of a corrupt social and economic order in to which the child is born and, against which, its birth offers a radical hope and alternative. This combination of liberal theological thinking and political analysis may seem fairly innocuous to a contemporary reader. Nevertheless one has only to recall the events of 1993, concerning the critical reservations that Bishop David Jenkins of Durham had in relation to aspects of religious orthodoxy, to suggest that elements of political and religious conservatism are still depressingly prevalent within British social and cultural life. The original production had been played in modern dress to foreground the play's contemporaneity. Unfortunately, there are no surviving photographs of that original production. The photograph shows a performance of the second, revised production at Ilkley Playhouse in April 1942, directed by Richard Ward. One of the alterations introduced into this revised version was the dress convention of stylised robes. The photograph features, from left to right, (standing) Wilfred Harrison, John Headley and Jack Boyd Brent. Left to right (kneeling) are Piers Plowman, Greta Newell, Phoebe Waterfield and Jane Fitzgerald. It is a matter of speculation as to why Ward, known and respected for his fiercely-held views, chose to amend the original script. My instinct and deduction is that under the difficult financial conditions under which the company functioned, Ward felt that they could not afford to lose a play from the repertory without another to immediately replace it. He was also sufficiently pragmatic and astute to recognise that a slightly revised version in performance was preferable to an original locked away in a drawer. Further evidence of Ward's theological and political analysis can be received from his [attributed] article in *The Adelphi*, June 1940:

> The first necessity for a new order is a recognition that it must be based upon Christian love ... This means that the earth, which is able to produce enough food and wealth for all, must be open to all peoples. An order of society based upon the opposite of this, that is, upon self-interest supported by violence or the threat of violence ... will be one in which the periodic massacre of innocent human beings and the exploitation of the earth in the interests of a few will be most likely to continue. [32]

These are essentially the sentiments that informed Ward's writing of this play.

---

32. Ward [attributed], 'A Tribunal Statement', *The Adelphi* (1940), p.370.

In terms of a first-hand account of, and response to the play, I had the opportunity during my research for this book to interview Canon Philip Lamb, the retired Principal of Ripon and St John, who remembered the play in performance. This production was at what was then his parish church of St Aidans, Harehills, Leeds in 1942:

> I can still see the scene in which Joseph and Mary come to Bethlehem. The Chorus stand in a line, shoulder to shoulder making a wall, the palms of their hands raised facing forwards ... They said in chorus:
>
>> Pretend not to notice, pretend to be asleep.
>> There is no room, no time, no will, no wish
>> Reject and prevent it;
>> It is not our affair.
>
> I found the rest of the play a little verbose and the action rather static. [33]

Lamb's description was recounted some forty years after the event itself, and yet the symmetry and ritualised movement that he describes is potentially evident, I feel, in the stylised grouping of the actors in the photograph. The photograph also indicates the effective and dramatic use made of limited stage lighting by the company, and one can imagine, perhaps, the impact of the stylised costume in the context of strong light and shadow. One newspaper review of the play in performance seems to reinforce this impression:

> This Nativity Play is akin to Greek drama in its production, relying for effect on the beauty of the spoken word and the eloquence of the mime. The actors' moves have pattern, and the contrasting timbre of human voices gives added meaning to what the words say. One sensed that the actors were imbued with the spirit of the word. [34]

Another reviewer of the published text of the play was less favourable and echoes Lamb's reservations regarding the allegedly stilted and overstated language:

> Here is the groundwork of a play only as far as speech is concerned. Religious, statuesque and sincere, but lacking in freedom and spontaneity, the words do not suggest action, they do not set the reader among people and events moving to a climax, they are devoid of humour. The men who have not looked for honour, for greatness, who have but hoped for the light to shine on them, the common ordinary people smile and laugh in their lives and are not real when only in long faces. [35]

---

33. Canon Philip Lamb, in recorded interview with author, Harrogate, November 1986.
34. *The Ilkley Gazette*, 27 November 1942.
35. *The Weekly Review,* June 1943.

Significantly perhaps, the second quotation expresses only a review of the written text rather than the play in performance. Equally, it is impossible to know whether the reviewer's reference to the 'common ordinary people' reflects either a stereotypical, patronising view of the working-class, or an informed defence of their own authentic culture.

After much careful consideration, I have to say that I do not believe that *Holy Family* is an outstanding play, although I do think that it is a very good and interesting example of its genre which, at one time in the early mid-century, had seemed – as Ward himself believed – to indicate the best opportunities for the development of new writing and theatrical form. However, in common with much, if not all, other verse drama of this century, it poses problems in terms of theatrical action. The play relies inevitably upon the dynamics of the poetic dialogue to compensate for the more diverse and complex interaction afforded by prose drama. My sympathies are with Auden who, in his 1938 speech in Paris, 'The Future of English Poetic Drama', asserted that:

> Poetry unalloyed tends, if one is not very careful, to introduce a rather holy note. You cannot have poetry unless you have a certain amount of faith in something, but faith is never unalloyed with doubts and requires prose to act as an ironic antidote. [36]

Another problem that the play faces, and one which the reviewer of the published text identifies, is the tendency for the human characters to become abstracted through the use of the poetic form. In his celebrated critique of the verse drama genre, 'Prose and the Playwright [1954], Kenneth Tynan succeeds in identifying the limitations implicit within this genre, and argues for the freedom and diversity of theatrical form which has been achieved through the seminal works of late nineteenth-century naturalism:

> The perfection of art in the theatre depends neither on naturalism nor on poetry. Drama in its time has borrowed tricks from both, but what it has built is a new and separate structure, whose foundation stones – the last acts of *The Master Builder* and *The Three Sisters* – are architectural triumphs of prose over naturalism ... Nobody wants to banish luxury of language from the theatre; what needs banishing is the notion that it is incompatible with prose ... Those playwrights who have followed the Ibsen/Chekhov lead are in the mainstream of modern drama. [37]

Ward had hoped that a play such as *Holy Family* might prefigure a new form of theatre that would embody a transformed theatre of the post-war period.

---

36. W H Auden, 'The Future of English Poetic Drama', in *Plays and Other Dramatic Writings by W H Auden*, edited by Edward Mendelson (Faber, 1989), p.521.
37. Kenneth Tynan, 'Prose and the Playwright', in *A View of the English Stage – 1944–63* (Davis/Poynter Limited, 1975), p.140.

Adelphi Players preparing backstage for their production of Strindberg's *Easter*. Directed by Elliot Martin Browne, 1942. Featuring (left to right) Richard Ward and Jack Boyd Brent. Photographer: Unknown.

However, with the first New Wave of writers in the post-1956 period including those such as Wesker, Arden and Bond, it was to be social realism as a broad genre, and a politically leftist-tempered humanism, that was to characterise its initial achievements, not the conservatism and Anglo-Catholicism of Eliot, Duncan and Fry.

3   Intimate Plays

Easter by August Strindberg. This production opened at the Central YMCA, Great Russell Street, London on 12 January 1942 and was withdrawn on 16 April 1943 at the Ilkley Playhouse after 64 performances. In his selection of this third generic sub-group for the company's initial repertory, Ward was clearly directly influenced by the establishment, by Strindberg and Falck, of the Intimate Theatre in Stockholm in 1907. Ward had stated that this category of play was intended for performance to small audiences, under conditions that might bring the actors into closer contact with their audience than conventional theatres might ordinarily allow.

   In a sense, one can view this as Ward making an aesthetic virtue of a frequently-encountered necessity. Also, a pragmatic business sense recognised that a play with latent religious symbolism would be well received in a number of the church-related venues that the company performed in at this time. Another interesting feature of this production was that it brought Martin Browne as a guest director from the Pilgrim Players. The plot of the play, both in its rather transparent religious symbolism and the delineation of its central characters, is essentially melodramatic. It may have been these potential shortcomings that led some reviewers to respond to the production in the following ways:

> Whether the jerkiness in the production was attributable to the difficulties of presenting Strindberg, or to the handicap of limited stage space is not easy to estimate. In dispensing with elaborate stage sets, they place additional emphasis upon the quality of their acting. [38]

And

> The largest part is that of the eldest son played by J Boyd Brent, who at times seems a little too theatrical in the role, but on the whole gives a pleasing and satisfactory performance. [39]

Another review illustrates how, albeit modestly, Martin Browne sought to experiment in this production by removing the 'fourth wall' from between the actors and their audience:

---

38. *Lincolnshire Echo,* 23 April 1942.
39. *Cambridge Daily News,* 12 March 1942.

> A somewhat unusual but effective device was employed in this play ... that was
> to have Mrs Heyt introduce her home to the audience and invite them to share in
> the Easter festivities of the family. [40]

A photograph of *Easter* in production shows John Headley, Greta Newell
and Jane Fitzgerald. Although it is difficult to deduce very much from this
photograph, one can see a glimpse of a simple, draped box set with either a
French-window or curtained fitting with a pelmet. This in itself indicates the
very simple form of setting imposed upon the company by necessity of cost,
transport and venues. At this time, and indeed through until the later
formation of The Adelphi Guild Theatre with a base of its own, the company
were working to a basic setting of hessian flats and drapes. That this stage
was cramped and small can be judged from the fact that, to the stage left of
Fitzgerald and thus to our right, the curtained area seems to end and the
stage left of the floor can be seen, possibly five to six feet away. From this
evidence, we can confirm, with reasonable conjecture, what we know from
other sources: namely, that The Adelphi Players were playing a venue that
shared common and predictable features – one which was probably not
intended for performance at all or, at the very best, one which inhibited the
professional presentation of theatre. In terms of the general practical day-to-
day business of touring theatre under these circumstances, Molly Sole was a
key and indispensable member of the Adelphis. Greta Plowman remembers:

> She was, for virtually the entire time of the company's existence, our secretary
> and 'Holder-Together' of the entire administration of the company. For the first
> number of years she remained in London because she had her job in London, and
> did her work for the Adelphis as a part-time job which was exceedingly taxing ...
> Eventually she did give up her steady job to become our full-time secretary and
> general administrator. We owed her a great deal. [41]

Molly Sole wrote about her involvement with The Adelphi Players in an
article entitled 'Theatre in the "Forgotten" Areas – The Story of The Adelphi
Players', published in the November 1945 issue of the magazine *Our Time*, a
journal loosely associated with values and issues relating to the broad left:

> In over fifteen hundred performances The Adelphi Players have put the works of
> Shakespeare, Webster, Ibsen, Carroll, J J Bernard, Synge and many others before
> the widest variety of audiences, a large proportion of whom had never before
> seen a "live" performance ... mainly in the mining and industrial areas ... By 1943
> the original company had compiled sufficient information on available halls and
> local demand to be able to work out three circuits which covered the whole country,

---

40. *Consett and Stanley Times*, 5 January 1943.
41. Plowman, in recorded interview with author, April 1990.

and each of these three areas are now [1945] toured once a year. At the same time the company adopted a policy of always carrying three plays in their repertory. By this means, a production is toured for at least a year but at the same time each area is presented with a fresh repertory as the yearly visit comes around. [42]

Sole's account provides useful information about the nature of the Adelphi's repertory circuit which compares interestingly with other 'models' of repertory, both historically and contemporary to the period. In their comprehensive account of the Repertory Movement, George Rowell and Anthony Jackson seek to define this important and integral strand within the development of British theatre:

The term 'repertory' is a much used and abused one and ... we should perhaps make clear ... the sense in which we are using are it. Strictly, a repertory theatre is one that stages its plays in rotation, building over a period of a year or more a store of productions that are offered to the public on a regularly changing basis, each play being performed no more than a week at a time but brought back at frequent intervals according to public demand ... Broadly, repertory theatres in Britain have seen themselves as determinedly non-commercial in approach, based in and serving a specific community or region and providing a wide range of plays, new and classic, challenging and popular ... Repertory, in fact, from the very beginning has been an idea in the minds of its advocates as much as it has been a practical method of presenting plays. [43]

It's perfectly clear that The Adelphi Players, and indeed the other companies under consideration, correspond to this concise and excellent definition of repertory theatre. Ward's commitment to providing theatre of quality and plays of artistic merit to audiences and communities who had previously been theatre-less, accurately reflects the pioneering and socially progressive nature of much of the best work in this area. Throughout their operation during wartime Britain they could count upon a steadily growing audience. As Molly Sole observed, they enjoyed particular support in those industrialised, urban areas where the WEA and the Co-operative Society had strongholds in local working-class education and culture. In terms of this section dealing with their plays in repertory and their own existence as a company committed to non-commercial, broadly progressive theatre, the following extract offers a clear indication of their values and aims. The extract is taken from a reported account of a 'Theatrical Brains Trust', based upon the immensely popular BBC Radio series of that period. This version of that programme format had been organised by the Hanley branch of the WEA in November 1943, to which the company had been invited:

---

42. Molly Sole, 'Theatre in the "Forgotten" Areas: The story of The Adelphi Players', *Our Time*, November 1945, p.70.
43. Rowell and Jackson. pp.1–2.

Question: 'Which do the Players think their most satisfactory audience and why?'
Greta Newell: The best audiences come from those whose working life is most
vital and has sharpened their sensitiveness, for example miners in South Wales
and County Durham.
Question: 'To create a theatre worthy of democracy, the man [in the street] must
be persuaded that the theatre speaks to his condition and that he not an outsider
in it. At present, the passion to build a truly National Theatre stirs only a minority.
How can this minority be increased until the movement is implanted in the life of
the nation?'
Jack Boyd Brent: It is no good building such a theatre of bricks and mortar before
it is built in the general life of the community. The people must know what they
want from the theatre, for it is the meeting place of their aspirations, and of the
enthusiasm of the players and dramatists. The Adelphi Players believe that good
plays must be taken to people everywhere. A National Theatre requires that new
dramatists arise to speak for their age. Audiences and players must meet, think
and talk together, feeling that they share the same co-operative enterprise. [44]

Boyd Brent's espousal of the company's aims in relation to both their
immediate work and also their commitment to a truly National Theatre, may
be seen and understood more fully in the context of the debate that had been
in progress since the turn of the century. Leading figures in this movement
included Shaw, William Archer and Granville-Barker, campaigning for a
National Theatre built on repertory lines. Early examples of repertory
excellence included Sir Barry Jackson's Birmingham Repertory Company
and the pioneering work of Miss Annie Horniman in Manchester, where
Lewis Casson and Sybil Thordike had begun their acting careers. At the
conclusion of the war in 1945, when CEMA was to be reconstituted as the
Arts Council, one of its major policy thrusts was to establish regional centres
of theatrical excellence, feeding and drawing upon local communities. This
policy decision clearly influenced The Adelphi Players to decide to settle as
a building-based repertory company in Macclesfield, serving the North West
Midlands.

Before proceeding to examine the formation of The Adelphi Guild Theatre
in 1947, it is necessary to deal briefly with an earlier rift and division in the
original company.

From the middle of 1941 when the original Adelphi Players had begun to
tour, they had spent about eight months performing essentially in and around
London. Initially they had two plays in repertory: Housman's *Abraham and
Isaac* and Ward's *Holy Family*. This situation developed with other plays,
including those under discussion in this section, being added to the repertory
through until early 1942. At about this time, there was a significant Company
Meeting called at which differences of personal and artistic opinion were

44. Hanley WEA-organised 'Theatrical Brains Trust', November 1943.

aired. As the situation in London began to ease somewhat after the intensity of the early months of the Blitz, short tours revealed demands elsewhere. In March 1942 a regional tour of six weeks initiated a period in which work in London alternated with progressively longer tours. The very first long tour included a visit to Ilkley Playhouse which, later, with the co-operation of its owners the Ilkley Players, became for some time the headquarters of The Adelphi Players. Another tour involved their involvement, in conjunction with local authorities, in the 'Holidays at Home' scheme. In September 1942 the company rehearsed for the last time at The Oaks and it was in the summer of that year that Ward advocated the winding up of the original company.

As it happened, the company continued for another twelve months with Ward's own play *The Heroic Legend of Robin Hood* acting as the final catalyst for tensions and difficulties to surface. To everyone concerned, the play seemed to be a thinly-disguised metaphor for the relationships and accompanying undercurrents within The Adelphi Players. Ward, Harrison and Waterfield submitted their resignations, to take effect from the end of the season in September 1943.

Simultaneously, Maurice Browne intervened, having been invited as a guest director for the production of *The Duchess of Malfi*. Browne had made his reputation in the United States of America where he is generally credited with having started the Little Theatre movement with his forming of the Chicago Little Theatre in 1912. He then went on to gain recognition in this country by producing the premiere of Sheriff's *Journey's End* in 1928. In 1930, he won critical acclaim as an actor for his portrayal of Iago to Paul Robeson's Othello. Clearly therefore, his arrival in the company represented someone with significant and wider theatre experience. Bettina Headley and Greta Plowman remembered the impact of his arrival:

> He taught us creation in rehearsal time, with his expert help we really sought the truth ... [45]

> He brought a whole new dimension to our playing, to our rehearsal, and Richard – although he so much wanted us to be a democracy, to conduct our own affairs – he did find it hard when we began to show signs of maturing and I think that precipitated the split ... although he [Ward] had some marvellous qualities and I always know what I owed him. [46]

Browne's arrival is not remembered in unanimously positive terms but the rifts were healed and, for a short time, Ward toured with a smaller Second Adelphi Company. It was the minimal resources of the Second Company that John Crockett took over to establish his Compass Players.

From his viewpoint, Ward wrote a retrospective article discussing his analysis for the split within the company. This article, 'The Adelphi Players

---

45. Bettina Headley, in recorded interview with author, April 1990
46. Plowman, in recorded interview with author, April 1990.

The Adelphi Guild Theatre Company, Macclesfield, 1947. The photograph features, from left to right, (back row) Frank Brown, Seamus Stewart, Hedley Lunn, Jack Boyd Brent, Cecil Davies, Rosalie Seddon, Ronald Sly, Valerie Gray, Tom Jellis; (front row), Piers Plowman, Penelope Barron, Wilfred Bidulph, Bob Threlfall, Greta Newell, Molly Sole. Photographer: Unknown.

– A Tabloid History', was published in *Peace News* on 29 August 1947:

> The company, almost without apparent warning, was rent by 'ideological' differences and split into two factions. These two factions sometimes called themselves (or each other) the 'artistic' and the 'sociological', but this was not really an accurate description of their differences. More truly, the majority wanted to get closer (with important reservations) to the established theatre, while the minority, to which I belonged, felt it had begun to break new theatrical ground, and wanted to experiment – with plays, audiences, methods of acting and production and staging. [47]

The Adelphi Guild Theatre

Using, though not uncritically, Ward's terms of analysis, it is nevertheless significant that it was the remaining majority within the company who made the decision to re-form and re-name themselves as The Adelphi Guild Theatre in 1945, after a short period of touring as The First Adelphi Company, with Boyd Brent and Browne assuming the joint roles of director. They continued to tour along the same basic lines of the original company. Their repertory ranged from *Bernice* by Susan Glaspell through Turgenev's *The Bachelor* and Ibsen's *Enemy of the People* to *Shadow and Substance* by Paul Vincent Carroll. Their final season before the move to Macclesfield was a successful repertory season in Cornwall in the summer of 1946.

In an article in March 1944, Alan Bendle, the theatre critic of the *Manchester Evening News*, had discussed the benefits that CEMA had achieved during wartime Britain to the encouragement of the arts. In this same article, he listed the total number of companies, including the two Adelphi companies and the Pilgrim Players, that CEMA continued to support. The list gives an insightful glimpse into the relatively diverse range of companies both active and receiving support: Sadlers Wells opera and ballet companies; Tennent Plays Ltd; Ballets Jooss; Ballet Rambert; the Birmingham Repertory Company; Stanford Holme Company; Norman Marshall Company; Travelling Repertory Company; Market Theatre; Walter Hudd Company; and repertory companies at Glasgow, Perth and Dundee.

This growth in theatre activities during the war had also been aided by the Government introduction, that same year, of fiscal laws which encouraged and rewarded commercial companies to finance touring productions by stipulating that they could avoid paying the Entertainment Tax providing that the touring work was defined as non-profit making. Also in 1945 the Government produced a White Paper on 'Community Centres' recognising the achievements of the non-commercial, independent theatre initiatives during wartime. Even more significantly CEMA became redefined and

---

47. R H Ward, 'The Adelphi Players – A Tabloid History', *Peace News*, 29 August 1947, p.5.

renamed in the following year with the object of:

> developing a greater knowledge, understanding and practice of the fine arts
> exclusively, and in particular, to increase the accessibility of the fine arts to the
> public ... to improve the standard of execution of fine arts and to advise and co-
> operate with ... Government Departments, local authorities and other bodies on
> any matters concerned directly or indirectly with these objects. [48]

One of the first initiatives of the newly-formed Arts Council was to encourage
and press for the development of regionally-based theatres. With the cessation
of war and the attempt by the authorities to resume more stable social,
economic and cultural conditions, this decision reflected a move away from
the support of touring companies, towards a policy of national, regional
restructuring that would facilitate the rebuilding of communities in the
immediate post-war period. This policy decision, coupled with an
understandable weariness after five years of touring, decided the Adelphis
towards plans for the creation of the Adelphi Guild Theatre.

After considering the offer of a former Miner's Hostel in Stoke as a base
for their work, they turned instead to Macclesfield where their work had
always been well supported. They had always received considerable support
from the local amateur dramatics society who gave the company the use of
their Brocklehurst Hall for performances and to rent as a rehearsal space. It
was on 12 February 1947 that they moved into their new, permanent base.
The name change was made because it was felt that 'Players' signified, and
was often synonymous with, amateur theatre. In their first prospectus The
Adelphi Guild Theatre stated that:

> The Adelphi Guild Theatre is the first step in a plan to develop a regional theatre
> in the Cheshire/Potteries/South Lancs area ... This plan is similar to the Arts
> Council's other regional developments ... It will be our policy to offer you as
> wide as possible a selection of the best theatre ... New playwrights, discussion
> groups, educational work, co-operation with amateurs ... We don't believe in
> ivory towers of smug seclusion. We believe that the theatre is part of a community
> and a part of the life of every member of that community. The plays we produce
> are in sympathy with that aim. [49]

The repertory for their first season was Ibsen's *Ghosts*, Priestley's *I Have Been
Here Before*, *The Duke in Darkness* by Patrick Hamilton and *The Moon in the
Yellow River* by Denis Johnston. Ted Willis went to see their production of
the Priestley play, reviewing it for the *Daily Worker* on 22 March 1947:

---

48. Ronald Hayman, *The Set-Up* (Methuen, 1973), pp.231–32.
49. The Adelphi Guild Prospectus, 1947.

The Adelphi Players ... have pitched their tent at last. I found the group of enthusiastic young actors and technicians pursuing the same aim – putting on good plays at reasonable prices in theatre-starved areas ... the people have taken them to their hearts and packed their house at all performances. They have not been disappointed. The production ... which I saw was a credit to all concerned. [50]

The late Ted – latterly Lord – Willis had established a reputation for himself as an activist within both the pre-war Unity Theatre and the ABCA Play Unit within the war. There were still some connections between individual company members and the ideological stance of the *Daily Worker*, with at least one member remaining an active member of the Communist Party. This informal association may help to explain Willis' attendance at what was a relatively unknown company in a new venture. Nevertheless, as encouraging as Willis' assessment must have been to the company, by 1948 there were undeniable rifts again. This time, they were forming between Boyd Brent, Browne and the rest of the company, over both the choice of plays for the repertory and what was seen as a diminishing standard in production. Company members such as Seamus Stewart were anxious that the broadly political left, socially progressive nature of the company should not be lost. Cecil Davies argued for the sustaining of the company's early, Ward-inspired ethos of a company centred on ethical and egalitarian lines. However, Boyd Brent was more concerned with the development of a more commercially sustainable repertory company. Increasingly, whilst the company had the use of their Macclesfield base and received a guaranteed sum against loss from the local authorities, local people began to perceive The Adelphi Guild Theatre as spending too much of their time and resources in touring to other venues and towns in the local region. In 1949 at their AGM, Boyd Brent was outvoted and removed from his post as Director and Stewart elected in his place. However, by this time, much had already been lost and undermined in terms of public goodwill, company morale and the overall artistic standard of the work. There was a recovery of sorts throughout the 1949–50 season although this was to be, paradoxically, their last full season.

Attendances had been deteriorating rapidly and matters finally came to a head early in 1950 with the Financial Sub-Committee having decided in the previous November that the subsidy – given as a £250 guarantee against loss – was not to be continued after the close of that season in May 1950. A vigorous campaign of letter writing and debate continued within the pages of the *Manchester Evening News*. More significantly, the Arts Council had, by now, withdrawn a grant of £500 to the company. Despite final, impassioned pleas, there was to be no reprieve and The Adelphi Guild Theatre went into voluntary liquidation in 1951 at the end of the season.

Thus came to an end an enterprise that had survived over a ten–year period and one which characterised a commitment to theatre as a means of social

50. Ted Willis, *Daily Worker*, 22 May 1947.

progress and human enlightenment. This ideal was tested by, and essentially survived, the extreme conditions and difficulties of wartime.

I shall review the Adelphi venture once again in my concluding chapter, but wish to end this study of their work with a final quotation concerning Richard Ward, expressing both the idealism and determined realism that characterised so much of his life and work:

> In conclusion [Ward] suggested that the proposal [for the Adelphi's work] was unlimited. This might be the first small beginnings of a great artistic revolution [or] ... nothing more than a gathering of people entertaining a pathetic illusion ... For himself he ... did not believe that this last explanation was true ... In this connection he quoted Auden: 'Hunger, work illegally and be anonymous.' [51]

---

51. The Adelphi Players Company Meeting Minutes, 1941.

4

THE COMPASS PLAYERS

In his article 'The Adelphi Players – A Tabloid History', written in 1947, Richard Ward recalls the final stages of the Second Adelphi Company:

> Times were changing; I at least was conscious of being exhausted in body and spirit. In some ways I think we were asking more of the public than we had a right to be. We finished up in London with three weeks of Raynall's great play, *The Unknown Warrior*, at the Lindsay Theatre. Very few people came to see us. But all I personally regret is that we lost money for some of our friends. This failure was the last straw however; we were in debt and had to go out of business. The Compass Players, who more than adequately carry on the 'revolutionary' tradition of the Adelphis, paid our debts and took over our assets. A couple of weeks later, the Arts Council voted us the extra grant which, had they and we known at the time, might have saved us. Irony was always a powerful feature of the theatre. [1]

This is a useful and pertinent quotation with which to open this fourth chapter concerning the Compass Players. The Compass Players were founded by John Crockett and his wife Anne in 1944. Along with the other companies under consideration, they shared an enduring commitment to an egalitarian lifestyle and a desire to take good quality, professional theatre to towns and villages where otherwise there might be none. Other significant features of this company was their commitment, although not across their whole repertory, to a highly visual physicalised style of theatre; and their particular relationship to the experimentation with community living.

In contrast to Martin Browne and Richard Ward, John Crockett's background was more grounded in painting and dance. He was born in Hampshire in 1918 and was educated at Bryanston School and Goldsmiths College School of Art. He also attended the Slade School to study theatre design, along with attending classes at the London Theatre Studio, founded and run by Michel Saint-Denis and George Devine. At Goldsmiths, Crockett studied under Polunin who had worked in collaboration with Picasso and Léger in designs for Diaghilev. The Theatre Studio was arguably to have one of the most extensive influences upon aspects of experimental approaches to performance in post-war British theatre, through both its application of contemporary European interests in mask work along with a more physical,

---

1.   R H Ward, 'The Adelphi Players – A Tabloid History', *Peace News*, 29 August 1947, p.5.

less cerebral, approach to performance. Saint-Denis had worked with his uncle, Jacques Copeau at the Vieux Colombier, and with his Compagnie des Quinze had worked on the premiere productions of plays by André Obey – whose work also featured in the repertory of the Adelphis, Compass and Century theatres. It is clear, I believe, that the combined influences of John Crockett's exposure to this style of working along with his, and his wife Anne's, dance training, was to play a central part in his artistic experiments with the Compass Players. Anne Crockett recalls the circumstances in which she and John had first met through her work as a dancer:

> We met when he had been persuaded to visit the Margaret Barr Dance Drama Group, of which I was a member. He was introduced to us by Freddie Manner, one of his teachers at Goldsmiths College of Art. Margaret Barr had been one of Martha Graham's pupils in the United States and had come to England in 1928 where she had worked at Dartington. From Dartington she had come to London and formed a group of professional dancers who used the special technique of Martha Graham, based on the natural movements of the body, unlike ballet. She composed dance-dramas and had the music composed specially for them, again unlike ballet where the opposite process takes place and the dance follows the music. [2]

In addition to his abilities and training in painting, design and dance, Crockett also gave his energy and talents to a centre for psychologically disturbed children at Little Missenden Abbey in Buckinghamshire, where painting was used as a form of therapy. Whilst there, he met Charles Brasch, the poet and dramatist whose play *The Quest* was to become an important part of the Compass repertory. Brasch remembered Crockett at that time in the 1930s:

> He was in violent revolt against his father's military tradition; his father was a regular army officer, his brother was destined for the army, and so had he been ... He declared himself a communist; his paintings [at that time] were full of caricatures of capitalists priests and soldiers, stock figures of the time ... he was so possessed by waves of inarticulate rage against the world in general and especially his own upbringing that he seemed like those figures in the Gospels who fall to the ground incapable ... before Jesus drives the devil out of them. [3]

This description by a close friend creates a vivid portrait of a young man consumed by both creative energies and waves of anger, particularly against his own, upper middle-class background. His other close friend, Richard Ward, shared similar traits, which may explain the incidents of conflict, at times, between the two men across their lifelong friendship. The combination

2. Pamela Dellar, ed, *Plays without Theatres – Recollections of The Compass Players Travelling Theatre 1944–1952.* (Highgate Publications Ltd, Beverley, 1989), p.3.
3. Charles Brasch, cited in Dellar, p.4.

of strong feelings and frustrations with the state of the world are revealed in
the following extract from Ward's letter to Crockett dated 28 February 1941:

> Dear John
>
> I have been working like a horse since I got back; that's my only excuse for being
> so damned rude – and the fact that I wanted to finish the Rilke (if one does 'finish'
> a book of that kind) and send it back with the letter. But I am sorry, all the same,
> not to have thanked you and Anne sooner for having me and giving me the
> opportunity to enjoy myself so much. That week ... was a good prelude to the
> kind of muck one meets here in London. Heavens! it is foul ... of all the loathsome
> and degrading occupations, sitting in your house waiting for a bomb to fall on
> you is the one that takes the biscuit. It's abject, it is passive; it is inhuman. That's
> the trouble with this war – you can't be heroic (I mean in the true sense of heroism,
> deliberately and positively doing the difficult and dangerous thing); you just wait,
> abjectly, for death, and it is a vile occupation not fit for human creatures ... Well
> anyway all I am saying is that I am very grateful for a week of remote Cornwall
> before I came back to all this and to work in it ... They can do what they bloody
> well like, take the bread from my mouth and the clothes from my back, but I'll go
> on trying to realise the things I stand for and they don't till I am so spent in body
> and will that I can't do anything but lay down and die. [4]

This extract from Ward's letter confirms once more the depths of frustration
and anger and frustration that both men felt about the destruction and waste
of the war, and its impacts upon their work and contribution to society as
artists.

The Cornish visit that Ward alludes to was connected to the involvement
of the Crocketts with experiments in radical community living at this time.
Community, of course, has become a much used and misused contemporary
term in both politics and the arts. Its employment within a reactionary,
Thatcherite vocabulary, for example, 'Care In the Community', has become
synonymous with a political culture similar to that envisioned in Orwell's
1984. In other words, language is used to conceal, invert, and rationalise the
self-interest of realpolitik strategies. 'Community', therefore, carries with it
latent associations of an assumed, pre-existing social group with a reactionary
ideological consensus. This Thatcherite model incorporates an inescapably
reactionary notion of a 'community-culture' defined by individual self-help
and self-reliance, dispensing with the need for either legislative and/or
financial support from the State. It must also be said that in its resurrected
use in liberal contexts such as Community Arts, its implicit meaning can
come perilously close to an uncritical, even nostalgic idealisation of, for
example, working-class or ethnic communities. One can see, perhaps, how
in terms of the complex, post-modern and post-industrial, western world,

---

4.   Richard Ward in letter to John Crockett, dated 28 February 1941.

that 'community' becomes a sort of talisman of the right and the liberal/left for a desire for an allegedly 'lost' past in which human beings could be identified and co-exist within a context of shared social, cultural and economic interests. In this seductive territory, devotees of Samuel Smiles and William Morris can enjoy an unlikely, but free, association.

In strictly etymological terms, the word has its root in the Latin 'communitas': meaning 'common', as in common possession or enjoyment. In terms of my own use of this word within this book, where I refer for example, to communities that were previously theatreless, I am employing the term to describe a local or regional geo-demographic constituency. An example of my use, therefore, would relate to The Potteries where, when visited by companies such as The Adelphi Players, there was a predominantly white, working-class skilled demographic complexion to this area. This centred on an extensive network of common employment in both the mass and specialised production of tableware and ceramics. As I have demonstrated, I am aware of some of the misleading assumptions inherent within contemporary uses of 'community'. In foregrounding my own socialist and quasi-Quaker ethical values, I am recognising my intrinsic gravitation towards a democratic and pluralistic model of the term. Clearly, whilst this issue is of importance and it is one to which I shall return in my concluding chapter, it is not possible within this chapter to pursue the debate concerning Community Theatre between, for example, divergent practitioners such as Ann Jellicoe and John McGrath.

Returning, therefore, to John and Anne Crockett and the Compass Players, there is a particularly interesting important link with a specific experiment in community living: the Taena Community. A version of this community is still in existence in Gloucestershire although it had its origins in Cornwall. Whereas The Oaks provided an initial base and ideological inspiration for Ward's initial company, the Taena Community was to exert a more long-lasting influence on the Compass Players. George Ineson, one of the founders of the community and who continued to live there, was a good friend and a close friend of the Crocketts, and he describes something of both the ideological and cultural background to the community and his first meeting with them:

> In the autumn of 1937 I began work in an architect's office ... In the evenings a friend and I were also discussing the possibility of starting a residential community on the outskirts of London ... one main fear was that it would become a clique of 'bourgeois intellectuals' because working-class people would find it too impractical to join; I felt he was probably right, and the whole idea was dropped ... [Nevertheless] the common denominator was a desire to discover a freer and fuller way of living ... [5]

---

5.   George Ineson, *Community Journey* (Sheed and Ward, 1956), p.25.

One can see from the sentiments expressed within Ineson's letter that the 'desire to discover a freer and fuller way of living' communicates a certain kind of radical liberal idealism inherent within that aim. From the latter decades of the nineteenth century, artists and reformers like William Morris, and movements such as the Pre-Raphaelite school of artists, embodied a selective and romanticised remembering of an allegedly idyllic, agrarian past. Morris believed that the craftsman required freedom from the constrictions and exploitations of capitalism and mass production. In 1884 he had founded the Socialist League in order to pursue and communicate his ideological aims. Furthermore, in prose romances such as *News from Nowhere* [1890] he sought to explore the interconnections between his socialist ideas and analysis, and his vision of a Utopian alternative to the industrial society of late nineteenth-century British imperialism. The Arts and Crafts movement which Morris pioneered led to the creation of new towns in the early twentieth century such as Letchworth and Welwyn Garden City. These were essentially suburban communities planned and built on the basis of such ideas from Morris and others. This emergence of an ethical, Fabian socialism led inexorably to the kind of thinking and initiatives supported by Middleton Murry and The Oaks. Furthermore, its insistence upon a re-marriage of the Arts and Religion, or Arts and Ethics, helps to contextualise the ideological position that people such as Ward and Crockett held.

An architectural assignment took Ineson to Cornwall and in 1938 he was married there. He and his wife, Connie, rented a small bungalow in Newlyn and invited many visitors there in the summer of 1939 just prior to the outbreak of war:

> Through the pacifist group, the Independent Labour Party and the anarchist movement, we met a strange variety of people forming a world of it own – a world of revolt against established order that autumn war broke out and ... horizons shrank to the problems of the moment; for us, this consisted of how to earn a living as pacifists in wartime, until such time as we were sent to prison – also working out what forms of pacifist propaganda were to be used. Public opinion naturally hardened against us as the war became a struggle for survival, and open-air meetings began to rouse violent opposition ... It was about this time that Connie and I went to London for the Annual General Meeting of the Peace Pledge Union; there was a minority who felt that the Union was ... compromising too much with a society that engaged in what we all believed was evil in its very nature. I remember a typical gathering of this minority; we all sat on the floor and between speeches ate sandwiches and drank beer; on the walls in large letters, had been painted Blake's dictum, "Religion is Politics and Politics is Brotherhood." [6]

---

6.   Ibid, p.30.

This quotation reveals, amongst other things, the diverse range of ideological positions within the PPU at the outbreak of war. The selection of a quotation from Blake carries with it, I feel, unmistakable resonances of that particularly native English vein of visionary non-conformism. In that tradition, included in which I would view the paintings of Samuel Palmer, the political vision seems to spring from a personal, revelatory experience. It is worth recalling at this point that Max Plowman, who had been the first secretary of the PPU, and was respected as one of the leading critics and commentators on Blake, had first met and befriended Ward through the PPU. It was also through the PPU and the ILP that Ward and Crockett had met. John and Anne Crockett had invited Ward down to Cornwall where they themselves were guests of George Ineson. Ineson had been given exemption from military service at a tribunal and he had started to explore means, along with other pacifists in that area, of earning a living. A self-sufficient community held strong appeal and, following on a visit and house search from the CID, Ineson and his wife were to meet Gerald Vaughn who was to play a crucial role in the establishing of Taena, and subsequently, the circumstances in which the Compass Players were formed. Vaughn came from an extremely wealthy family who had made their money out of the global tobacco business. He lived a rather remote life and subscribed to pacifist views. His home was a modest smallholding that was adjacent to where the Inesons were staying. He had already given generously to a religious pacifist community known as the Society of Brothers. Ineson continues his account of that time:

> His [Crockett's] political beliefs were a cross between anarchism and socialism similar to our own ... he generously suggested that we should start on his small-holding of eight acres to which he had already added an adjoining smallholding of five acres. We accepted this offer and set out on our community journey in September 1940 ... About three months after we had started the community, we met John, Anne and Bettina. We first saw them taking over possession of a cottage ... and we discovered that we had much in common and began to discuss the possibility of them joining the community, which they did early in the summer of 1941. This was the situation that existed correspondingly to Ward forming The Adelphi Players. [7]

The community outgrew the facilities that Vaughn's smallholding could provide and so, whilst Crockett went to visit Middleton Murry at The Oaks for advice and help, the rest of the group temporarily dispersed. It was at this time, towards the end of 1942, that Crockett was invited by Ward to join up with the Adelphis, whilst Anne Crockett went to teach in Lancashire whilst Bettina – later to join The Adelphi Players herself – worked on a farm in Devon. The Inesons continued to provide a base 'in transition' in Cornwall and Crockett wrote to them whilst on tour with The Adelphi Players:

---

7.   Ibid, pp.32–4.

If you and Connie still want to go on [looking for a new base] I should be very willing to start again in a new place if that is physically possible. Further, I shall join you all as soon as possible if you were all willing and there's a farm to live and work on. As it seems unlikely now that anything will turn up now before Michaelmas that will probably mean staying on with the Players until then, a matter about which I can't say anything definite until I see Richard which I hope will be this week. [8]

The search for a new community base finally resulted in a farm becoming available in the Cotswolds. Named The Warren, Gerard Vaughn again provided the capital, buying it and leasing it out to the Inesons and the community. The community members moved in during September 1943. Earlier in that same year, and corresponding with the divisions and split within the original Adelphi company, John Crockett had decide to try and form a separate company himself. There were two main motivations for this. Firstly, whilst Crockett and Ward were close friends, their strong personalities found it hard to work together within the one company; secondly, Crockett was concerned to try and develop a more physical, visual and dance-related company in contrast to the more literary, text-based approach of Ward and The Adelphi Players. Accordingly, whilst Crockett's sister-in-law, Bettina Stern, was to join the Adelphis, and marry John Headley, the Crocketts formed the short-lived Adelphi Dance Company. Dancers were auditioned and the composer Peter Burden agreed to join the seminal company. CEMA were prepared to support the project on condition that work permits were awarded by the Ministry of Labour. A number of the prospective dancers had come to England from Germany with the Ballet Jooss. However, the permits did not materialise and the venture ended prematurely. Nevertheless, the Crocketts were undeterred and the concept of the new company was translated, in the following year 1944, into the formation of the Compass Players.

Simultaneously, there were differences of perspective and temperament between Crockett and Ineson in terms of the exact nature of the community that was emerging, with some tensions, at The Warren. Ineson had written to Crockett in the autumn of 1943 to try and indicate that Crockett might not easily fit into this problematic, emerging community. Crockett replied to Ineson on 28 October 1943:

I gather that you now have 'a nucleus of five who can live together even at close quarters harmoniously', and that you 'feel that additions to this number must only take place after people have found in practice whether they also fit it' ... you have doubts whether we'd [he and his wife] fit in because I'm too concerned with my career, and that any concentration of thought towards painting would hinder

---

8.   Crockett, cited in Ineson, p.44.

the Group ... Personally, my mind has been oriented for the last nine months on re-joining you, and I have always understood from you that there was reciprocation in this ... Whenever I was on tour, and people got talking to me, my answer was always "Oh, I am only temporarily with them [The Adelphi Players]" ... and that has been made clear over and over again to the Players ... I have also made it clear in all my dealings with the Dance Co that as far as I am concerned, my regard towards it has only been temporary, and that as soon as I had got over all commitments, I would be departing thence. [9]

Whilst efforts were made on both sides to resolve the issue of the relationship of the Crocketts to the embryonic Taena Community, by the summer of 1944 conflicts had reached a head. As an integral part of a creative resolution to the dilemma, the Crocketts decided to build upon their experience with the Adelphi Dance Company and in the autumn of 1944 formed the Compass Players. The foundations and strengths within the relationship between George and Connie Ineson and John and Anne Crockett proved stronger than the tensions they had faced over Taena. Therefore in 1946, when two original members left Taena, John Crockett asked if it might be possible for the Compass Players to take over The Warren and use it as a rehearsal space and permanent base. Ineson recalls in retrospect:

This took place in 1946 and the strange relationship between the opposites of the Compass Players and the Taena Community became an important element in the lives of both groups. Every three or four months the company would take up residence, and strange declamations would reach us while we were milking the cows, ending with the excitement of the week before the first performance ... Woven into all of this were the periodic experiences of a new Compass Players production. These had a magical quality difficult to describe – partly due to knowing everyone concerned, partly to the unusual approach to acting, and partly because of the kinds of plays they chose to perform. One production which I remember very vividly was *The Quest*, a dance drama written by John and his friend Charles Brasch and danced to the Fantastic Symphony by Berlioz. [10]

Further tensions and conflicts, perhaps inevitably, would emerge towards the end of the company's existence, but the Compass Players continued to have its base at The Warren from 1946 through until their demise at Easter in 1952.

Before examining the circumstances in which the company eventually folded, I shall consider and discuss the structure of the company, its repertory, and most significantly, its performance style.

---

 9. Crockett, cited in Ineson, p.48.
10. Ineson, cited in Dellar, p.156.

The Compass Players: Structure, Repertory and Performance Style

John Crockett borrowed £150 from a friend and took over the assets of the former Second Adelphi Company and preparations began in 1946 for establishing the Compass Players. The contributory aesthetic factors of John Crockett's imaginative theatre design and painting, his exposure to the physical theatre and mask work of the Theatre Studio, and Anne Crockett's absorption of the contemporary experimental dance of Martha Graham, were all to be of crucial significance in the development of their performance style, and to some extent therefore, the repertory of the company.

This background also helps explain the inclusion of regular daily dance / drama workshops which served as warm-ups for company members Such a practice, which although current and common practice today in both Drama Schools and theatre companies, was relatively rare in Britain at the time. Anne Crockett recalls those sessions:

> Many of our programmes, such as the story of the Fool through the ages called *The Jester*, had as much dancing and miming as speech, but even for those plays that had no actual dancing, I insisted on the company doing drama technical exercises and lyrical movements daily. These were based on breath control. Drawing in the breath and holding it gave the accent and tension, breathing out gave relaxation, and 'following through' a completion of movement. Doing these exercises greatly improved an actor or actresses's timing ... it gives meaning to a phrase as in music the placing of the climax gives shape to a musical phrase. [ll]

The company, as with the Pilgrims and Adelphis, were egalitarian in structure with equal wages for all company members. Martin Heller, who joined the company in January 1948 and remained until its closure in April 1952, recalls his initial involvement:

> My first job was basically that of ASM and my only part was in *The Last Enemy* where I played Death. After that I played: Lieutenant in *Man of Destiny*, Cléante in *The Misanthrope* and Faustus in *Dr Faustus*. Members of the company received fifteen shillings per week but had no living expenses – food and accommodation and necessary clothes being provided from general funds. This system also applied whilst on tour. [12]

Also in common with the Pilgrims and Adelphis, the company often relied upon the hospitality of locals when touring further afield as Armine Robinson, an actress with the company, recalls:

---

11. Anne Crockett, cited in Dellar, p.29.
12. Martin Heller, in written correspondence with author, 14 November 1986.

> Every time we came up to this part of the world [the North East] we came here
> [Ormesby Hall – now a National Trust property] to live while we toured around
> places like Bishop Auckland, the convent in Whitby ... Ruth Pennyman [the owner,
> during the period, of Ormesby Hall] loved the theatre very much and she had
> [Joan Littlewood's] Theatre Workshop based here in 1946 and other companies ...
> the Pilgrim Players also came here. [13]

Pam Dellar and Armine had shared digs together and become good friends
whilst training as actresses at the Central School. At the successful conclusion
of their training, Pam Dellar had gone off to work with the Compass Players
whilst Armine, through her agent, found herself in the throes of touring rep.
It is worthwhile quoting from her recollection of that time, giving as it does
such a vivid, first-person account of touring commercial repertory at that
time:

> The job turned out to be in Blackburn at a twice-nightly weekly rep ... I arrived at
> the Grand Theatre in time for the first performance of *Jane Eyre* ... It was quite
> dreadful ... when the orchestra suddenly launched into melodramatic music at
> the entrance of Rochester's mad wife I wanted to go back to London! ... The next
> few weeks were incredible. We presented a different play every week with
> performances at 5 p.m. and 8 p.m. each night ... I learnt my lines more or less
> accurately, but found the 'cue scripts' we often used extremely unnerving. It was
> a nightmare only to have one line (or less) of the speech before my own (the cue)
> printed on the page. There was no indication of how many other people had
> spoken since my character last said anything or what had been going on. There
> were two married couples in the company who played the older 'character' parts
> and had trunks filled with useful props, wigs and bits of costume. They knew all
> the traditional 'business' for plays like *East Lynne* and were very helpful to me
> when I found myself playing Lady Isobel (a huge part) for two performances
> only during the last week of the season! [14]

As it happened, the Compass Players visited the Grand at Blackburn with
their own production and, after seeing a matinee production of their *Pardoner's
Tale*, she was invited – and agreed – to join the company. There are several
important issues that arise from Armine Robinson's recollections. Firstly, one
receives a sense of the eclectic nature of touring theatre at this period, where
companies such as the Compass Players, with their experimental blend of
progressive theatre, were playing at the very same venues as the stock
company which Robinson found herself with. Secondly, in terms of her
experience, it would seem that little had changed in terms of the playing
conventions from that of the fictional Vincent Crummles immortalised in
Dickens' *Nicholas Nickleby*.

---

13. Armine Robinson, in transmitted interview with BBC Radio Cleveland, 1990.
14. Robinson, cited in Dellar, pp.68–9.

Consequently, Robinson reveals an assortment of old and dated costumes and props, to be used quite pragmatically by aging actors who had learnt the standard 'business' for a particular number of 'stock' parts, and melodramatic music to sign any significant 'dramatic' occurence on stage. George Rowell identifies the same prevailing characteristics in his discussion of the stock companies of the nineteenth century. Nevertheless he also asserts that not all examples of this kind of theatre were as inept as Dickens' fictional example:

> As an apprenticeship to acting the stock company was rich in experience if poor in pecuniary reward ... Actors knew their 'line' if not their lines, and borrowed dialogue from one play for another without the audience's knowing or their colleagues suffering, provided they 'came to cues'. Indeed these colleagues rarely noticed the loan, since they were supplied only with 'sides' (long sheets of manuscript) which revealed their own lines and the preceding cue. [15]

Clearly these kinds of theatrical conventions could not afford the time, scope or, frankly, the necessity, for character exploration in rehearsal or performance. Nevertheless such companies did provide the actor with equally invaluable skills in terms of versatility and improvisation. The company which Robinson briefly worked with must have been one of the last survivors of its kind. One can understand the attractive alternative that a company such as the Compass Players would represent for a young actress. Not only was there the more interesting and challenging repertory, but also the relatively long rehearsal periods which allowed for creative experimentation and investigation. Finally, there were the multiple challenges and attractions of living within a company committed to a communal existence.

The itinerary for September and October 1951 shows three plays in repertory: *Time's Fool* by Holberg, *Strange Return* by P D Cummins and *Dr Faustus* by Christopher Marlowe. Ludwig Holberg [1684–1754] was a Norwegian-born writer who spent most of his working life in Denmark. His significant contribution to Danish national theatre was to write and produce plays for the first time in a vernacular and comedic style. Influenced by Molière, his work is not well known in this country and in fact the first major translation of his works only appeared in England in 1957. It is an indication of the experimentation and eclecticism within their repertory, that the Compass Players should risk a production by an author who, at that time, would not have been seen within the British theatre of the period.

With their production of *Dr Faustus*, the company had chosen a play which had been one of the mainstays of the original Adelphi company. It also serves as an important example of a Compass production that characterised their commitment to an interactive use of dance, movement, mime, mask and

---

15. George Rowell and Anthony Jackson, *The Repertory Movement: A History of Regional Theatre in Britain* (Cambridge University Press, 1984), p.8.

Masks made by John Crockett for use in the Compass Players' production of *Dr Faustus* by Christopher Marlowe, featuring Hedley Lunn in the role of Faustus. This production was directed by John Crockett. Precise date and location unknown but the year is 1950. Photo: John Crockett. From the collections of the Theatre Museum. By courtesy of the Trustees of the Victoria and Albert Museum.

music. The masks that Crockett designed and made for the Seven Deadly Sins for this production offer a telling sense of the stylised, visual impact of this production. The photograph on the facing page of the masks in use in this production reveal a potent, heightened theatricality. The photograph features Hedley Lunn in the role of Faustus. With their combination of early twentieth-century Expressionism and the Byzantine medieval, the masks point unequivocally to Crockett's undoubtedly powerful, visual aesthetic. The masks were made out of papier mâché and tailored to fit the faces of the individual actors. One can also see from the photograph that in order to enhance the masks' effectiveness and practicality, they were worn in conjunction with head-dresses.

These were made from hessian on a wire frame. Whilst the photograph seems clearly to have been stage-managed or choreographed, it still evokes, I believe, a strong sense of the stylised vocabulary of the company in performance. The late Maurice Daniels, an actor with the Compass and later with the Century, remembered the production as, in his opinion, one of the best pieces of work which the Compass Players produced:

> John managed to pull together that disparity of talent into a kind of integral whole, which meant that every member of the company went on stage to perform to their highest endeavour ... he was splendid on text, he had 'an eye' and would 'eagle in' on the spurious ... If you're not alive at every moment on stage ... then the scene is going to have an emptiness. It's the integrity that comes through the shared experience, and we most certainly learnt that from John. [16]

Whilst this assessment of the production, and Crockett's abilities as a director, was made some forty years later and is inevitably subjective, Daniels was drawing upon subsequent and extensive experience with the RSC following on from his work with the Compass and Century companies. Experimentation of the sort associated with the *Dr Faustus* production represented an avant-garde departure from the mainstream within British theatre of that period. It therefore marks a particularly exciting initiative in terms of a small touring company playing non-standard venues. I have no formal evidence that Crockett saw any of The Group Theatre productions of the pre-war period in which Doone experimented in similar vein. However, I believe that the similarities in performance language and genre are potentially persuasive indicators. In interview, Pam Dellar felt personally that such a connection was possible, if not probable.

The music for the production was taken from Strauss. Every company member was involved as a performer with much doubling or tripling of parts. One journalist who reviewed the production described the manner in which they were able to achieve this formidable task:

---

16. Maurice Daniels, in recorded interview with author, Stratford upon Avon, June 1987.

To see the production from the auditorium was itself a delightful experience; to see the actors fulfil their multiple roles ... behind the scenes ... was such an insight into what good comradeship and a real community of purpose can achieve in the arts ... When the Seven Deadly Sins perform their mime before Faustus and Mephistopheles the entire cast has to be (or seem to be) on the stage at one and the same moment. Who then would control the intricate symphony of illusion in light and sound which was a vital part in the play's success? Sloth, whose movements on stage were the embodiment of inertia and weariness, was for one moment concealed in the wings. In that moment he took on the attributes of Mercury. He moved with astonishing alacrity from dimmer to gramophone. He adjusted the lights, changed the record, set the music of the ballet in motion, and at the right moment re-assumed the character of Sloth and with infinite weariness took his place at the tail of the procession. [17]

With their production of *The Quest* by Charles Brasch the company again took the opportunity to use mime and movement in a stylised manner within the realisation of this verse drama. The play bears some similarities in style to Ward's *Holy Family* and, interestingly, it was Ward who was invited to direct the original production which opened at Kingston Church Hall, Herts, on 1 April 1946. As Brasch says in his introductory note to the published text of his play:

The play is an experiment in combining the drama of words and the drama of movement. About half the action is conveyed by the words as printed and about half by miming ... The play was written for a small travelling company of actors, The Compass Players, whose director, John Crockett, provided the sketch of a plot to suit their requirements and giving scope for both kinds of drama ... the result is thus a joint production. [18]

With one central character of the Shepherd, there are five other performers, who, as in *Holy Family*, serve as Chorus and also emerge as individual characters. Unfortunately, to my knowledge, there is no surviving visual evidence of the play in performance. I believe that it shares the same generic shortcomings of *Holy Family* whilst, again as with that play, remaining an interesting example of that genre of religious verse drama. I want to quote from the opening passage of *The Quest* in order to communicate a flavour of the poetic verse dialogue and the interchanging of the collective and individual dramatic voice:

MAN: Turning –
MAN AND TWO WOMEN: Turning –

---

17. T E Bean, 'The Compass Magicians', *Halle Magazine* (1950), p.30.
18. Charles Brasch, *The Quest: Words for a Mime Play* (The Compass Players, London, 1946), pp.5–6.

CHORUS: Turning of the timeless wheel of the heavens,
               Systems and suns and generations
               Are borne through momentary light into
               Unanswering darkness,
               Borne into time and out of time,
               Massing in memory and still pursuing,
               Pursuing the memory of what has gone before,
               The shadow of what is not yet come,
               By that unquestioned master driven,
               Unquestioning need
               In universal pulse –
MAN: Rocked by the rhythm of –
WOMAN: Lured by the love of –
SECOND MAN: Tossed in the tumult and –
SECOND WOMAN: Slipping from the summit of –
CHORUS: (Diminuendo) Time – time – time – time.

The play continues with the theme of the human journey and quest for an inner, spiritual/psychological truth, using the Biblical narrative of the shepherds visiting the Christ-child as a metaphor and means of exploration. In its style and with its latent preoccupation with the resolution of internal conflicts within the human life journey, the play reflects, I believe, many of the contemporary concerns facing both Crockett and the Taena Community. In a letter from Crockett to Ineson contemporaneous to this period, Crockett attempts to analyse some of his fundamental struggles:

> One must live in the world and therefore cannot reject it. One must learn to accept. Perhaps a man is never so lonely as when he is with other people – for myself, I never feel so alone as when I am with people I care for, and usually unlonely when I am by myself. The world is like a flame with the greatest heat and the most intense beauty near its heart ... I believe mystics can experience that flame and its centre – but I am no mystic. I believe that to a certain extent the ecstasy is to be found here and anywhere in the diversity, perversity, beauty, and horror of life and living. [19]

Tensions continued to exist to one degree or another within both the Taena Community and the 'adopted' Compass community. These were to eventually contribute to the break-up of the company. It is interesting to note that whilst Crockett remained, effectively, an atheist at this time, he and his wife – along with some other company members – were eventually to be admitted into the Roman Catholic church. Many of Crockett's later paintings following on from that time explored religious symbols and icons. As productions such as *Dr Faustus* and *The Quest* reveal, I believe, there was,

---

19. Crockett, cited in Ineson, pp.56–7.

THE COMPASS PLAYERS

'SETTING FOR "A PHOENIX TOO FREQUENT" DESIGNED BY JOHN CROCKETT'

John Crockett's set design (pen, ink and watercolour) for The Compass Players production of *A Phoenix Too Frequent* by Christopher Fry. Sketch dated JC 49. From the collections of the Theatre Museum. By courtesy of the Trustees of the Victoria and Albert Museum.

in their texts and interpretations, a powerful, sub-textual struggle within both Crockett and the community being explored and defined.

Finally, one other play from the Compass repertory that is of interest is Christopher Fry's *A Pheonix Too Frequent*. As I mentioned in my earlier chapter concerning the Pilgrim Players, it was Martin Browne who commissioned this play from Fry for the Pilgrims' short season of verse drama at the Mercury Theatre in 1946. It was, in fact, this play and its production that helped to establish the reputation of Fry in the post-war period. The play came into the Compass repertory in the 1948–49 season in its own right and remained part of a double-bill throughout 1949–50 and 1950–51. The play and its author were still relatively new to the public and its inclusion and continuance in the repertory reflects the play's popularity. The photograph of Crockett's set design for this production shows the effective use that Crockett and the company made of the limited resources available to them. Dated 1949, the sketch – executed in pen and ink – incorporates the use of the portable hessian screens that the company had inherited from the Second Adelphi Company and the simple use of rostra to present a stylised and imaginative setting. The design reminds one again of the imperative that the Compass faced of creating settings for their productions that were visually interesting, inexpensive to produce, whilst remaining adaptable to differing venues, many of which would lack conventional stage facilities.

Schools' Work

An important, and in some respects, innovative aspect of the company's repertory was their Schools' work. Of course, on one very pragmatic level, the work was invaluable as a source of reasonably dependable and regular income. Nevertheless, it was not only the economics of survival that took them into schools, but a genuine desire to make theatre more accessible and relevant to young people, the potential theatre-going audience of the next generation. With very rare exceptions, it was not until the work of Brian Way and his work at the Theatre Centre in the mid-nineteen-fifties and onwards that the theatre specifically addressed the needs and interests of young people in relation to theatre. Whilst it is true that companies such as the all-female Osiris Players took their single-sex productions of Shakespeare's plays to schools during this period, this was a fascinating exception, rather than the rule. [20] Significantly, the original impetus for the Compass educational work came from the short-lived Second Adelphi Company, who in 1946 had proposed 'Demonstration Work in Schools'.

---

20. The Osiris Players were an all-female touring theatre company, who performed exclusively in schools during, and immediately after, the war. Whilst boldly subverting the Elizabethan performance convention of all-male casts, the little available evidence suggests that the company's aims and intentions were, surprisingly perhaps, rather more pragmatic and reactionary.

A copy of their summary syllabus is provided in Appendix C. It states as its general aim 'To stimulate interest in stage plays, and to encourage an appreciation of their acting, production and purpose'. With Crockett and Ward sharing a close friendship and views on the value of purpose of theatre, it is not surprising that, when the Second Company folded, the new company built upon the invaluable foundations that Ward and his small company had established. In a programme note from 1948, Crockett made the following policy statement in relation to their schools' work:

> The value of the Company's work in schools, apart from the excellent reports it receives in *The Times Educational Supplement*, can be assessed mainly by the fact that the demand for school performances increases yearly, and it is to meet this increased demand, for instance, that Marlowe's *Doctor Faustus* is being retained in the repertoire for another season ... Public Schools, Grammar Schools and Education Authorities alike have expressed their appreciation of productions which not only bring to life ... English dramatic literature that might otherwise have remained as purely academic experiences for school children, but to do so with considerable theatrical skill and thus reproduce the essential values of the play ... This, the Company feels, is a justified demand and one to which the theatre must accede if it hopes to combat the spoon-feeding effect of the cinema and help in creating lively and intelligent citizens of the future. [21]

Whilst the company were never to engage in any of the various forms of participatory Theatre in Education projects that were to characterise some of the outstanding TIE work of the nineteen-seventies and early nineteen-eighties, they did attempt to do more than simply provide a performance of the play – as valuable as that was in itself. For example, the following extract comes from the briefing notes for a Day Workshop/Drama School in relation to their popular production of *Dr Faustus*, given at Durham on 26 February 1952:

> The emphasis of this Drama School will be on play interpretation, and imaginative translation of a script ...
> MAURICE DANIELS: Talk on the creation of character, from conception to realisation in a production.
> ARMINE SANDFORD: Talk on mime and masks – how it feels behind a mask, and purpose and practice of conveying thought and feeling by movement alone.
> JOHN HOSKINS: Discuss co-ordination of stage-management, with the main emphasis on light and music plotting.

---

21. The Compass Players, Programme Notes, *Comus*, 1948 (kindly loaned to author by Martin Heller).

Compass Players – The Final Phase

At the close of their 1949–50 season the company was able to refer to what a critic in *The Times* had said of their work:

> The Compass Players look both forward and back, reviving old traditions and experimenting with new forms ... they have remained true to their aim of working in theatreless districts ... they run their organisation co-operatively for they are completely united in their respect for their work ... Perhaps Londoners may never see them, but at least they can be glad that such a company exists.

Nevertheless, in 1951, various problems were conspiring to lead to the eventual collapse of the company the following year. There were the almost inevitable difficulties within relationships, brought about by the close proximity within both theatre and community life. Furthermore the financial problems habitually associated with a small theatre company continued to beset them. Pressures specifically upon the relationship and finances of the Crocketts led to John Crockett resigning as Artistic Director in 1951, with Martin Heller being invited to succeed him. Sheila Louden, the company secretary based in London, was having serious difficulties at the same time in her discussions with the Inland Revenue regarding charitable status for them. Various new administrative procedures were required including the formation of a Board of Management which was to consist of John Crockett, John Headley and Richard Ward. Martin Heller describes the final sequence of events that led up to the collapse of the company:

> While Sheila was sorting out the Inland Revenue ... added to this a new home for the company had to be found, as the owner of The Warren ... was also in financial difficulties and needed to sell it ... John had also given notice that he wished to withdraw the guarantee of £300 which he gave to the bank to cover the company's overdraft. This proved impossible to replace and when it was finally withdrawn in February 1952 the fate of the company was signed and sealed. [22]

In a diary entry of 13 January 1952, George Ineson had written:

> The Compass Players, which carried on under another director when John retired, has run into further debt and will be closing up at Easter. John and Anne, who are both under instruction at the Abbey, have asked to come with us when, and if, we move. [23]

---

22. Heller, cited in Dellar, p.149.
23. Ineson, p.179.

The Crocketts did, in fact, follow the Inesons to their new, and extant, base at Whitley Court near Prinknash Abbey in Gloucestershire. Crockett continued to work in the theatre, though he devoted his time more exclusively to his painting. He ran a small theatre company called Ikon which did seasons at the Lyric Hammersmith in the early nineteen-sixties. Then after some freelance work as a director for the BBC – including the early series of *Dr Who* – he took up a permanent post at Downside School, becoming Director of Art there in 1969. His paintings were exhibited in one-man shows in London and Oxford, whilst others are in collections around the world, including that of Princeton University in the USA. His costume and set designs, masks and theatre drawings are in the permanent collection of the Theatre Museum in Covent Garden.

The Compass Players represented both a continuation of the broader ethos that motivated Richard Ward and the Adelphis, and Martin Browne and the Pilgrims, whilst marking a different direction stylistically in productions such as *Dr Faustus*. In their use of mime, masks, music and dance, their experimental performance style prefigured much of the significant Physical Theatre of the nineteen-eighties: for example the work of DV8, Théâtre de Complicité and Trestle Theatre. Also, in their early attempts at theatre for young people, built upon some of the proposed work of Ward's Second Adelphi Company, they prefigured the development of this crucial area in the nineteen-sixties and seventies. Their initiative was partly motivated and given impetus by the wide-ranging implications of the 1944 Butler Education Act. In its stated intention of providing secondary education for all children, and therefore providing more equality of opportunity, the Act required the formation of Local Education Authorities to administer the new system.

By 1948, the Compass Players could list 16 of these new LEAs under whose auspices they worked, and ten Public Schools, ranging from Ampleforth through to Cheltenham College. As Christine Redington remarks in *Can Theatre Teach?*:

> The Compass Players ... like many Community and Fringe companies now ... worked as a co-operative ... The company began to take performances to schools and this became an important part of their policy ... This approach was welcomed by schools and Education Authorities who recognised the value of bringing to life ... dramatic literature which might otherwise have remained purely academic exercises for the school children. [24]

Following John Crockett's death in 1986, there was a major retrospective exhibition of his paintings at the Westminster Cathedral Gallery which drew many people and to which I was invited. Finally, I wish to conclude this chapter with a quotation taken from Martin Heller. He sums up the aims of

---

24. Christine Redington, *Can Theatre Teach?* (Pergamon, 1983), p.35

the Compass Players and also reaffirms their conviction that good theatre can be produced from limited resources:

> The idea was to take plays of quality to areas which normally would have no chance to see them, in productions which were imaginative and exciting and as well presented as limited resources would allow. Excellence need not, and indeed does not, only reside in large companies with everything to hand, including money. Very good work can be done in small halls with poor facilities provided the imagination and effort is there ... there was no political input that I was aware of – just a belief in the value of drama itself. [25]

25. Heller, 14 November 1986.

5

THE CENTURY THEATRE

The formation of the Century Theatre represents the final, formalised embodiment of the broad aims, ethos and output of the companies from Martin Browne's Pilgrim Players, through Richard Ward's Adelphi Players and the Adelphi Guild Theatre, to John Crockett's Compass Players. It also represents the creation of, quite literally, a touring theatre in a way that has never quite been paralleled either before or since. In this chapter, I shall endeavour to describe the circumstances under which the concept of this unique touring theatre evolved. Furthermore I shall provide an account of how it came to be built under the extreme difficulties and austerities of post-war Britain. Finally, I shall examine the extent to which those aims and ideals expressed through Ward's Theatre of Persons were extant, if at all, and realised in the company structure, repertory and practice of the Century. In my discussion of the company, I am dealing specifically with the early years of its existence, up until the departure of Wilfred Harrison. After this time, I will argue that the chronological and thematic thread that ran from 1939 to 1951 ceased to exert any real influence upon the company and diffused into other directions.

All of the companies discussed in the previous chapters were firmly in the tradition of the travelling players. This tradition can be traced historically in the English, indigenous, popular cultural tradition through the medieval and Elizabethan periods, to the actor-manager-led troupes of the later eighteenth and nineteenth centuries. These continued into the twentieth century with such celebrated exponents such as Sir Donald Wolfit with his touring productions of Shakespeare.

Wilfred Harrison himself had worked with Wolfit's company as a young actor. Sir Donald Wolfit [1902–68] was with the Old Vic from 1929 to 1930, and after appearing at Stratford in the 1936 season formed his own touring company in 1937. During the war, he had given many lunch-time recitals of readings from Shakespeare and continued to tour Shakespeare around the country. In her dissertation, 'The Role of the Strolling Player in British Theatre Development', Sarah Jane Harrison observes that:

It is quite probable that some old-style strollers would still be at work in the early twentieth century; for example, in Cornwall and rural Wales. The World War brought a new need for the travelling players. C Neish Duncan describes his portable booth, The Garrison Theatre: "My theatre travelled in four loads. Two of the loads became the stage wagons. The wagons had floats on them and when spread gave a good-sized stage. The other two wagons were the gallery ... We played six pieces weekly, with the bioscope and lantern slides thrown in as extra. We used to stand about four to six weeks in one place, and if I may say so never played the same thing twice (maybe just as well) ... I was the first to travel an electric generating set in place of paraffin lamps." [1]

This extract is of especial interest and relevance within this chapter, representing as it does, a form of touring theatre still in operation only forty years or so prior to the formation of the Century. Furthermore, the function of Duncan's wagons as both staging and seating reflects exactly that unique aspect of the Century Theatre itself. Of course the example cited by Harrison was only one of various other travelling theatres. Consequently, both the range of repertory and performance was varied:

> ... in November 1901 [the same period that Duncan's Garrison Theatre was in operation] the columns of the theatrical paper, the *Era*, list 143 touring companies on circuit ... Several of the touring groups offered the same attraction, particularly the popular musical comedy ... while Mrs Bandmann-Palmer, an actress brave or rash enough to tackle Hamlet, was in her 'Thirteenth-Year of Tour with Company' ... Of course it would be unjust to condemn the touring system on the strength or weakness of its ... too too solid female Hamlets. [2]

The phenomenon of the actor and theatre as travelling and transient, rather than static and building-based, provides a continuing and appropriate context in which to view all of the companies covered in this book. This has particular resonance to the Century Theatre. Wilfred Harrison refers to the popularly acclaimed actor, Roger Livesey, in terms of both his helpful support of the Century project and also of his own travelling theatre background:

> Roger Livesey came from a family who were what had been called 'King Pole Players' – you'll realise that means they performed in a tent. His grandfather was a King Pole Player and there were many famous theatrical families that were in that tradition. With Roger having come from that stock, this idea of a mobile theatre intrigued him ... he was really most helpful. [3]

One of the strong and abiding characteristics of the companies under examination was, of course, their commitment to a concept and implementation of a communal existence. Therefore, one of the overriding

---

1. Duncan, cited in Sarah Jane Harrison, 'The Strolling Player in British Theatre History', unpublished dissertation, submitted as part-requirement for the BA (Hons) Combined Studies, Worcester College of Higher Education, 1985, p.11.
2. George Rowell and Anthony Jackson, *The Repertory Movement – A Study of Regional British Theatre*, (Cambridge University Press, 1984), p.12.
3. Wilfred Harrison, in recorded interview with the author, April 1988.

factors informing the formation of the Century Theatre was the perpetuation of that shared communal identity and lifestyle, with the added advantages of a well-equipped and purpose-built theatre. Its founders hoped and believed that this would offer practical advantages in terms of company accommodation, and also in the raising of production standards.

The extent to which that same sense of commitment to the company as a community, and the broadly shared idealism at its centre could be maintained in the social and economic climate of post-war Britain was to prove to be a fundamental issue. It necessitated a growing dependence upon commercially reliable plays in repertory, as is raised in the following recollections of Maurice Daniels who joined the company from the Compass Players:

> Richard [Ward] knew my work, Wilfred knew my work. I believe that Richard was going to direct *Othello* originally and so they invited me to join the company to play Iago initially and to be the Publicity and Tours Manager. At the centre there was an abiding sense of community and idealism because there was Wilfred, myself, Peter Smallwood – although he would have been in the commercial theatre – was very much a kindred spirit, Pheobe Waterfield ... In addition to them there were one or two young actors. It was not the same as Compass or Adelphi – in terms of quality of plays, yes, but with more compromise towards audience acceptance – we were dependent on box office. With the Compass Players we were guaranteed a fee. It was a movement towards more conventional Rep, although we did Marcel's *A Man of God* which had a good storyline but also a deep philosophical and moral dilemma within it. [4]

Daniels' evaluation naturally reflects his own subjective memory and interpretation of the company's ethos and repertory. It was certainly true that the Century did have to rely more so on revenue from its box office. In that important and pragmatic sense, the Century might be said to represent a 'movement towards more conventional Rep'. However, following close examination and comparison of the repertory across the repertories of the Adelphi, Compass and Century, there is actually considerable similarity between them.

In view of the interchange of personnel between the companies and their broadly shared ethos and raison d'être, this is hardly surprising, of course. With building-based theatres becoming gradually re-established again in the years immediately following 1945, and receiving prioritised attention and financial support from the Arts Council, the pressures upon the Century to remain financially viable whilst also retaining its artistic integrity were considerable. Nevertheless, the Century reaffirmed the integrity and ideals of its aims in a four-page manifesto published as early as September 1947:

---

4. Maurice Daniels, in recorded interview with author, June 1987.

The Century Theatre is not being formed solely as a theatre capable of moving from place to place. Its primary aim is the presentation of plays in as high a standard of performance as is necessary for their proper appreciation. The plays in the repertory will be of indisputable merit ... The theatre is intended for the service of the community, and will be fully mobile in order to extend this service over a wide area. It will be a non-profit-making organisation; any surplus income after meeting expenses will be devoted solely to the furtherance of the theatre's work. The company will in itself be of a co-operative nature; duties will be shared, salaries equalised, and a decent standard of living and the ability to meet personal responsibilities will be guaranteed to all members. [5]

Both Daniels' recollections and the Century manifesto reveal important aspects of the continuity of ideals and aims from the Adelphi and Compass enterprises, along with the practical pressures of a gradually increasing reliance upon plays that would be commercially viable.

Nevertheless, I believe that it became increasingly difficult to sustain those egalitarian and artistic aims and principles within the wider context of the inevitable social, cultural and economic changes of post-war Britain.

This is an issue which I shall discuss at greater length in my following, concluding chapter. Daniels felt that the sense of community was not as distinctly felt in the Century Theatre as it had been in the Compass Players. Whilst this is, of course, only one person's reflection, after a period of over thirty years, it might also indicate the differing perspective that accrues with the wider span, maturity and disappointments of life experience. Additionally, the attraction and significance of community life and egalitarian principles may have seemed undermined after the painful and disappointing circumstances in which the Compass company had folded. Furthermore, the wider social climate, with its remembered wartime ethos of popular, collective solidarity and comradeship, was fast disappearing. Clearly, the complex factors which contribute towards, and define, the processes of social change should not be oversimplified. Certainly, the period from the massive Labour victory of 1945 to its eventual defeat in the election of 1951, was one characterised by initial reserves of optimism and expectancy, to be replaced by a sense of exhaustion and disillusionment. The hopes for social progress and political change had been dealt a serious blow, as Anthony Howard writes:

Labour was fighting the symbolic battles and not the real ones. Its slogan in the election had been "Let us Face the Future"; its practice in Parliament was to correct the outstanding arrears of the past ... it merely indicates the difficulties which lay

---

5.   'The Century Manifesto' cited in Alan Hankinson, *The Blue Box: The Story of the Century Theatre* (Melbeck Books, 1983), p.13.

in wait to ambush the 1945 Socialist electoral dream. They may have not been insuperable, but they were certainly not overcome. [6]

The period of time during which the Century Theatre was conceived and, after much hard work and effort, materialised, coincides with that period of potential political radicalism and optimism, which was to end, conversely, in exhaustion and a climate of reactionary pragmatism.

Under the influence of social dislocation, transference of conventional labour roles and material shortages which characterised wartime Britain, companies like the Pilgrims and the Adelphis had found new audiences at non-conventional venues, eager for the recreation, distraction and stimulus of theatre. That interaction of ideological idealism, practical initiatives and a social need heightened by those social circumstances, inspired Ward and Harrison to build the Century Theatre in the post-war period. The process and means by which they, along with the engineer and designer John Ridley, achieved their aim is the subject of the following section.

The Blue Box: The Century Theatre

Much of the practical support that emerged for the building of the theatre came in the form of – literally – nuts, bolts and even the paint donated for the travelling lorries and trailers. The painting of the vehicles as they were gradually constructed took place under dreadful conditions in a dilapidated aircraft hangar in Leicestershire; a sorry left-over from the war:

> The colour they were applying to the aluminium was 'Chelsea' blue, which lies somewhere between the rival shades of Oxford and Cambridge. Walpamur gave the paint and offered them a limited choice. They had opted for the blue because an advertising man told them it had 'the greatest eye-catching effect' ... Distinctive it undeniably was ... and it provided the theatre with a nickname, the 'Blue Box' which has proved as durable as the colour. [7]

The people responsible for the initial concept of the Century Theatre were Richard Ward, Wilfred Harrison and John Ridley. At that time, 1947, Ridley was the Chief Engineer with Sketchley's Dye Works at Hinckley in Leicestershire.

The Working Men's Club in Hinckley had been a fairly typical venue for both the Adelphis and the Compass, and Ridley had seen the Adelphis' work, and met Ward and Harrison, in that context. Harrison recalls:

---

6. Anthony Howard, 'We are the Masters Now', in *Age of Austerity: 1945–1951*, edited by Michael Sissons and Philip French (Oxford University Press, 1986), p.19.
7. Hankinson, pp.17–18.

> I do remember [both he and Ward] being mightily impressed by his [Ridley's]
> engineering skill in transforming an ill-equipped stage into one congenial for our
> performance. John Ridley had earlier assisted Basil Langton's Travelling Theatre,
> a CEMA-supported company that toured the halls, centred on Birmingham, and
> it was his experience with the company that led him to the mobile theatre notion. [8]

Remarkably, Ridley had been working independently on his plans for a
mobile touring theatre. He was an excellent draughtsman and designer and
therefore, when he showed and discussed his ideas with Ward and Harrison,
they were impressed. The circumstances seemed auspicious for a perfect
timing of theatrical will, idealism tempered with experience, and technical
engineering and design skills. In terms of the actual construction of the mobile
theatre, Ridley worked primarily with two other men whose enthusiasm,
commitment and engineering skills were indispensable: Norman 'Rob'
Robinson and Richard 'Dick' Bull. Robinson had known the Ridleys some
ten years before and had been involved with the Compass Players along
with his wife and actress Armine. He was persuaded in March 1950 to join
John Ridley who had already been working since the beginning of 1948 with
Dick Bull. Bull was a skilled coachbuilder, who had been unemployed in
1948 when he joined Ridley. Harrison recalls Bull's significant and invaluable
contribution to the project:

> He was vital to progress, his knowledge and skills matching John's, not only in
> execution of plans but also in modifying them into practicality. He continued
> with the theatre on tour for four years as Chief Engineer responsible for erecting,
> dismantling and maintenance. [9]

Ridley had himself tried to work upon the construction in his own spare
time in 1948 whilst still maintaining his full-time employment at Sketchley's.
When this proved to be impossible, he resigned from his well-paid and secure
job, in order to work full-time for the embryonic Century for the weekly
wage of £2. He also used a considerable amount of his own capital to buy ex-
service trailers which were to become, quite literally, the foundations for the
travelling theatre. The material for the structure was aluminium which was
donated in large quantities by a Birmingham company, Birmetals Ltd. A firm
in Leeds sent a generating plant worth £2000. Norman Robinson recalls the
circumstances under which they worked from 1948 through until early 1952
when the theatre was finally assembled and ready for use:

> I worked on anything that John thought I was capable of, but I was slow and
> over-methodical compared with him. I did a lot of the electrical work. I remember
> that the floor and wall heating panels had to have their terminations contained in

---

8.   Wilfred Harrison, in recorded interview with author, 31 October 1990.
9.   Harrison, correspondence.

boxes filled with pitch, which I had to melt in a saucepan on the gas ring in the Waterworks' office, then running as fast as I could back to the theatre before it solidified again. [10]

Whilst Ridley, Robinson and Bull worked away under those primitive conditions in Hinckley, Harrison was busy publicising the venture and in the process seeking support through financial contributions or gifts in kind. In 1949, he arranged for a model of the Century Theatre to be displayed at the British Theatre Exhibition in Birmingham. Dame Sybil Thorndike who, as I have discussed in earlier chapters, supported both the Adelphis and Pilgrims, was a visitor to the stand, as was the well-known critic Eric Keown who recalled later in an article for *Punch*:

> To some of us it was the most exciting thing ... the young men ... said very sensibly that large parts of this country, particularly the rural areas, were now starved of professional theatre, and that there was a new and urgent need for [theatre] prepared to offer villages and small towns a genuine repertory of good drama ... All they had was this model and their determination to build their theatre with their own hands and take it round England as soon as possible. I think even the most sanguine of us came away with a few reservations, but there was something about those young men that warned us not to be too knowing. [11]

Meanwhile, the building continued in Hinckley whilst Harrison, having secured an ex-Army motorbike, continued on his series of ever increasing, circular journeys, with Hinckley as the constant, returning, reference point. Because materials did not always arrive when required, the building process was invariably haphazard. Harrison kept a record of all donations and gifts in kind and the following is taken from one of those surviving inventories:

> 30kw generator, 2,600 yards of electric cable, 2,200 square feet of hardboard, canvas for stage cloth, cyclorama and stage flats, 142 pieces of crockery, 72 tablets of soap, 2 doz bulldog clips, 6 typewriter ribbons, 10,000 staples and machine.

In retrospect Harrison reckoned that the gifts in kind probably amounted to a total of about £5,000 of the total cost of £25,000. These represented very substantial amounts of money indeed at that time. He estimated that:

> Of the money subscribed, most was in comparatively small sums; 15 guineas to endow a seat, but a mere half-crown was accepted with grace, and the donations came from a true cross-section of the population. Whilst it is true that Arts Council support was none during the building, there was government money from the Development Commission, a statutory body concerned for the welfare of rural

---

10. Hankinson, p.15.
11. Eric Keown, cited in Hankinson, p.16.

communities. They also gave the largest individual sum: £5,000. There was also a
£1,000 loan (interest free) from a Hinckley manufacturer and another such loan
from the then Dean of Worcester Cathedral, where the Adelphis had played several
times. [12]

As Harrison points out, in addition to the larger sums of money and gifts,
there were many other individuals, both ordinary people and celebrities,
who made their own contributions. In a progress report that was issued by
Harrison in August 1950, from which the following extract is taken, one gets
a remarkable glimpse into the diversity of people who supported the project
in various ways:

> The widespread requests for performances indicate the great opportunity awaiting
> the Theatre. The large numbers of applications for membership make it clear that
> a well balanced company can be collected. But in order to finish the work of
> reconstruction, £3,000 is needed (in addition to the working capital). Every
> donation or loan, however small, plays a highly influential part in putting the
> theatre on the road.

There then follows a long list of supporters, from which the following are
selected:

Abbeystene Women's Institute
Sir Ernest Benn
Miss Enid Blyton
Burlington Hotels Ltd
Miss Agatha Christie
Miss Cicely Courtnedge
Professor Bonamy Dobree
Sir Laurence Olivier [13]

The list has a diverse – almost eccentric – eclectical quality to it, ranging as it
does across such an incredibly diverse range of groups and persons. I believe
that it reflects something significant within the mood of immediate post-war
Britain. Almost an extension of the war years themselves – and with many of
the material deprivations continuing – this inclination towards a belief in a
changed Britain with increased educational and cultural opportunities helps
to explain the support and interest shown in the seminal company. The
common hope, no doubt encouraged by the propaganda of government
departments, was that such projects might help to create a more democratic,
just and culturally active society following the war. In this sense, the
conception and building of the Century Theatre represents a truly popular

12. Harrison, correspondence.
13. Ibid.

and egalitarian achievement. As Keown observed at the time, we too should not allow the doubtful benefits of both hindsight and a more jaundiced political and cultural weariness, to underestimate the scale of the achievement based on widespread popular support. In a newspaper article of the period, written by T C Kemp for the *Birmingham Post* [1950], the closing quotation from *Hamlet* evokes that mood of popular cultural patriotism, a sentiment which Suez and ensuing events would largely extinguish:

> I was astonished at the fine substantial craftsmanship and the expert technical planning that have erected on four great ex-RAF trailers the stage, auditorium and dressing rooms. The four sections open out and link up into a raked floor with 225 tip-up seats each of which affords a clear view of the stage. I saw one of the six caravans in which the company will travel and live. The company of twelve will feed communally in a canteen on wheels; water will be carried; and electricity will be generated on the site. Last Thursday, as I stood in the fading light in the shadow of the completed part of the Century Theatre, I wondered what it is about the drama that impels young people to give up well-paid jobs, live on a bare subsistence allowance and work like galley-slaves in order to provide good plays for theatreless communities. As I gazed at this outward and visible sign of a dream shaped into reality by courage, sacrifice and sweat, I was reminded of Hamlet's 'Good my Lord, will you see the Players well bestowed. Let them be well used; for they are the abstracts and brief chronicles of the times'.

In 1950 the venture was put on a legal footing with the founder members being: John Crockett, Wilfred Harrison, John Ridley and his wife, Richard and Jenny Ward; and two other former Adelphis: Phoebe Waterfield, whose career traversed the Oxford and Canterbury Pilgrim Players, the Adelphis; and, finally, the indefatigable Molly Sole. The following year, 1951, saw two other former Adelphis, Piers Plowman and John Headley, arrive with Molly Sole to start the actual painting of the theatre. Sole remembered 1951–2 in the following terms:

> It was the only winter I ever spent with the entire soles of my feet covered in chilblains ... when we committed ourselves we reckoned five months would see the job done. In fact it was nearly a year we spent in that hangar. Wilfred Harrison appeared once a week on this ex-Army motor cycle with our 'wages'. Occasionally visitors were brought to see the progress to stimulate Wilfred's fund-raising. I particularly remember Joyce Grenfell bravely climbing unfinished steps and gazing round, her eyes shining with approval. By then we had most of the theatre sections erected in the hangar so the seats could be bolted in. It was a great moment when the backs came into operation and the 'floor' became vehicle sides with the seats remaining in place and they really did 'nest' in as designed. [14]

---

14. Hankinson, p.17.

In the early months of 1952, the four main trailers which were the basis of the travelling theatre were completed, although the design concept now needed to be crucially tested in practice. Everything proceeded as Ridley had anticipated and further work continued through the summer of 1952. In late September of that year, the theatre was dismantled in its hangar and taken to the grounds of Hinckley Technical College, where the vast process of reconstruction took place. Alan Hankinson describes how:

> John Ridley wanted to reassure himself that the structure was strong enough not only to hold a full house but one that was in a state of excited enthusiasm. One afternoon a few days before the first performance he filled the auditorium with 225 teenagers from local schools and got them to jump up and down while he crawled about underneath the floor, among the jacked up wheels looking for signs of stress. [15]

A Utopian Theatrical Democracy

The title for this section of the chapter is taken from an article about the early Century Theatre, written by Dennis Holman for the *Illustrated News*. The same article features a photograph of two young company members cooking in the company kitchen. One of them was Eileen Derbyshire, who was to eventually find popular fame and recognition in her role as Emily Bishop in the long-running Granada television soap *Coronation Street*.

The other person featured was a young actor called Ross Wilson, who went on to become an ordained minister in the Anglican Church. Having enjoyed some success on the commercial repertory circuit at the time, circumstances led to him meeting with the Century Theatre on tour in Warwick:

> My brother had found this strange theatre in caravans in the park at Warwick. I wandered in and there was Wilf Harrison ... and I just chatted to him ... when Wilfred offered me the job – taking over from Maurice Daniels ... Of course, I benefited a great deal; you were living in a community which is good and everything was expanding because a lot of things were expected of you other than just acting. It did have a very special sense of community – apart from Maurice, all the 'founding fathers' were there ... and so there was this very strong sense that we were all part and parcel of the theatre and this very strong sense that we were serving the community. [16]

The sheer logistics of getting, and running, the theatre on the road were considerable. Maurice Daniels, Tours Manager and Iago in the opening production of *Othello*, remembered the miscalculation about the time needed

15. Ibid, p.22.
16. Arthur Ross Wilson, in recorded interview with the author, June, 1987.

for travelling and setting-up prior to a run. It was only when they were actually on the road that they realised how much more time was required than they had optimistically calculated:

> I booked a tour on the basis of that theatre going up in twenty-four hours and coming down in twenty-four hours. After our opening at Hinckley, it took us three days to put it up! I then had to re-jig the whole tour. We would close on the Saturday, open the next play on the Wednesday and then play a week or ten days. There used to be a three-day gap for travelling. With a hundred-foot trailer behind you, you could not go whizzing along at sixty miles per hour! [17]

Henry Livings, the writer and actor, also remembers being a young company member and recollects, with some humour, the reality of the demanding day-to-day existence on the road:

> We were a scruffy lot. Well, so would you be if you spent days in muddy fields or grit-blown lorry yards, winding up Crossley wagons, manoeuvring the side panels to stack them inside the trailer sections for the road, humping the blocks of wood that supported the hydraulic jacks, hauling at the tow bar ... As I recollect, a smaller trailer such as the box office, or the toilets, would be attached after one of the big theatre sections; and this was the tail that would come waltzing out from behind an apparently sedate caravanserai, taking up another foot or so of road space either side, at anything over 22 m.p.h. or in response to a vigorous swing of the steering wheel. The lettering on the side of the theatre, you may imagine, becomes a jigsaw when you dismantle. This intrigued passing motorists; they would gaze up, trying to interpret RY THE or EATR or whatever. [18]

Both of these first-hand, primary source accounts are interesting because they signify two contrasting aspects of the early company. One refers to the shared sense of community and idealism that still existed within the enterprise, a continuation from the earlier companies. Equally, Livings' recollections reflect, with humour and pragmatism, upon the sheer hard work and sense of commitment that was involved in moving the travelling theatre around the country. Ross Wilson continues this insightful glimpse into the living and working conditions, and the various jobs that one might be expected to do in the course of one, very long, working day:

> Breakfast was done by the members of the community in rotation and there was always a list of what sort of morning tea each company member had ... I was always a cook so I did not get involved in doing the washing up. We always

---

17. Daniels.
18. Henry Livings, from an article originally submitted for 'Century Anniversary'. The original document loaned to the author by the kind permission of the late Henry Livings, in correspondence with the author, July 1989.

peeled the potatoes – Henry Livings and myself – we'd be doing the cooking listening to 'Housewives' Choice' ... It was worked out that one had one third of the day free, one third doing whatever one's responsibility was, and of course in the evening you were involved in the production. If you were not involved in the production then you'd be Front of House. At any given time there'd be three productions in repertory: one to 'drag them in', one to satisfy the schools and one of a kind that was not going to be done anywhere else, for example, Strindberg's *The Father*. [19]

One final reference in this section to the experience of working within the company and the diverse demands it made upon its members, is highlighted in the following extract from a letter by Harrison many years later. In it, in which he responds to enquiries made by a research student examining touring theatre, he outlines some of the various responsibilities that cast members had in the opening production of *Othello*:

> IAGO: also Tours Manager and Driver and Publicity Manager.
> CASSIO: also a Senator, also member of the dismantling crew.
> DESDEMONA: also chief auditorium cleaner; also driver's mate; on box office rota.

That ethos of sharing tasks, a willingness to perform any menial job, what Pam Dellar described in retrospect as almost a 'messianic zeal', had threaded its way through from the earliest years of The Adelphi Players and The Pilgrim Players. Whilst the Century Theatre could not – and would not have wished to – claim to be either Utopian or even entirely democratic, in its daily existence, it did seek to maintain both its ideals and commitment to artistic integrity and standards. I shall consider this central factor in more detail in the context of their opening production.

'Their Common Ideal Is Art'

Once again, the heading for this section is taken from the Dennis Holman article. With the theatre now constructed and complete, the company having legal status, plans were made for the opening production which was to be *Othello*. Casting was already underway when Richard Ward fell seriously ill with a stomach ulcer. Having achieved the seemingly impossible in building the theatre, it now looked as if there might not be an opening production. Harrison recalls the anxieties of that time:

> Richard Ward was sick and was unable to do anything or organise that first production. Tyrone Guthrie had been very interested in and supportive of the Century. I had worked with him and I wrote and asked if he would direct the

---

19. Ross Wilson.

first production. Although he was unable to, he wrote back and recommended a young director: Abraham Asseo. He was sold on the idea, so he and I organised auditions. Abraham became a good friend and did other productions, he played a large part in establishing a standard of presentation. [20]

Asseo, who died in 1992, was remembered for his contribution to the company in the obituary written by Wilfred Harrison and published in *The Guardian* on 6 February 1992:

Perhaps it was Asseo's youthful experience in a kibbutz that made him fit easily into the Century community of players; but his warm good humour and enjoyment endeared him to his fellows, and his sure knowledge of what 'worked' on stage commanded their respect and admiration. After *Othello* he frequently guest-directed productions, including Strindberg's *The Father*, Molière's *The Miser*, and André Obey's *Sacrifice to the Wind*. [21]

Later in life, when Head of Radio Drama in Tel Aviv, Asseo remembered the circumstances in which he was drafted into the new company as director:

Our little flat in Warrington Crescent in London became a work room full of sketches for costumes and sets, and a stream of actors calling to be auditioned for the various parts ... The selection was made with an eye to fit the special character of the company – the actors had to be able to live together in a communal life, getting equal wages (technical staff and cook included) all sharing the same living quarters, meals in a common dining caravan, and having to give a hand with the mounting and striking of the theatre when moving from one place to another ... We rehearsed mornings, afternoons and evenings in ideal conditions, for all lived together on that site in Hinckley. There was an air of enthusiasm and great expectations all round. That, however, put me on guard for I feared that it might be confused for professionalism or minimise artistic discipline. But that did not happen. [22]

Even with the arrival of Asseo to resolve the problem of the director, a further crisis seemed imminent with the sudden collapse through illness of Harrison – cast to play in the leading role – two weeks before opening night:

It was an apprehensive time in personal relations – nobody knew the director, nobody had worked with him. I was playing Othello and then went sick – I got flu – the strain of all the preceding months finally got on top of me and I collapsed.

20. Harrison, interview.
21. Wilfred Harrison's obituary for Abraham Asseo, 'Kibbutznik with a stage presence', *The Guardian*, 6 February 1992.
22. Hankinson, p.24.

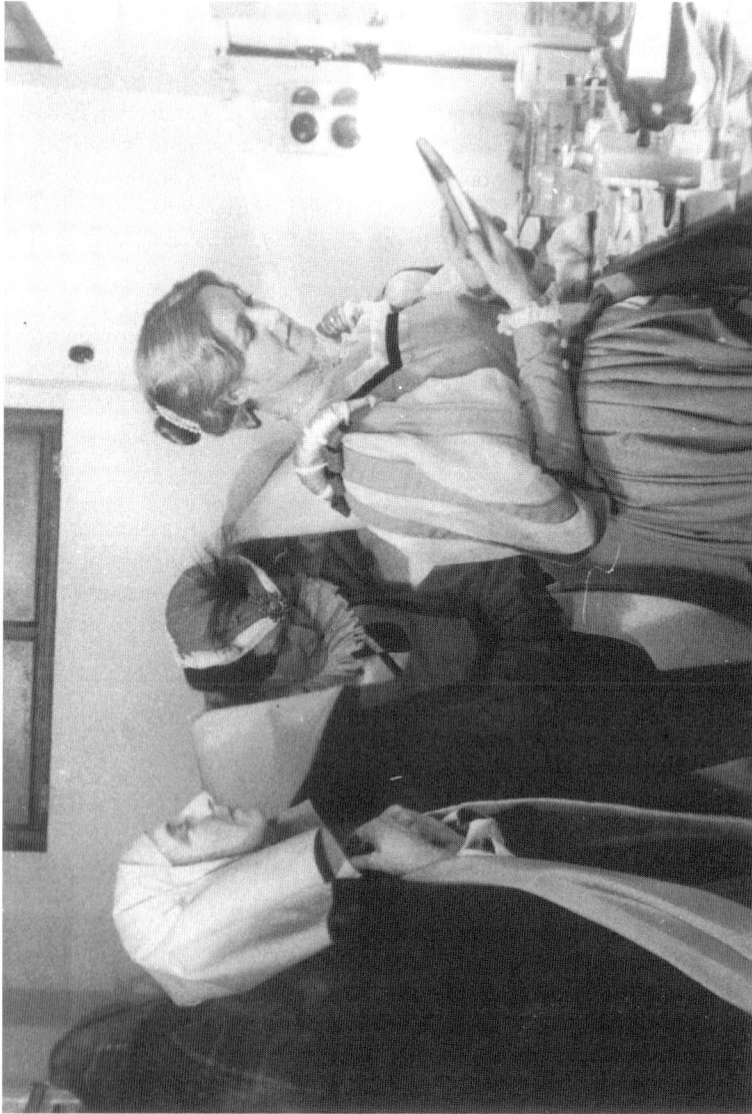

Actors in preparation for the opening production of the Century Theatre: *Othello* by William Shakespeare. The photograph features Phoebe Waterfield (left), Pamela Dellar (centre) and Norma Shebbeare (right). This production was directed by Abraham Asseo. Photographer: Unknown.

The opening performance was cancelled for a week, we opened a week later on 29 September 1952. We played in the grounds of Hinckley Technical College for a week and then the adventure really began – we were off on the road. [23]

The opening night attracted wide and extensive media interest with radio, as well as press, television and newsreel cameras, arriving to cover the event. There was obviously as much interest in the technological innovation of the theatre itself although those equally interested in the production on stage responded favourably:

> ... an audacious venture in taking plays to the people ... this *Othello* is a memorable one by any standards ... a production well worth going to see. [*Manchester Guardian*] ... From the moment the threshold is crossed any sense of impermanence vanishes. There is a wholly unaffected freshness in the work, and the cast seems to have reached the kind of unity which grows out of real and disinterested appreciation of their material. The whole caravanserai is a triumph of engineering and also of stubbornly courageous conviction. [*Times Educational Supplement*]
> ... It would have been a production of more than passing interest in London. It was smooth, vigorous, a model of team work ... Wilfred Harrison's Othello was outstandingly good. [Eric Keown, *Punch*]

Early in 1953, Marcel's *A Man of God*, directed by Ward, came into the repertory at Worcester and was followed by Molière's *The Miser*, directed once more by Asseo, in the middle of that same year. The initial, positive critical response to Othello was confirmed by the review by the correspondent of *The Times*, on the opening of *A Man of God* [the first British production of a play by this French playwright], who commented:

> It is altogether a better play than London has seen lately, and a courageous choice that does credit to this adventurous theatrical community. [24]

The repertory for that first Autumn tour consisted, therefore, of *Othello*, *A Man of God* and *The Miser*. The two adjacent photograph pages offer visual evidence of two of these three plays in performance and also of conditions backstage.

The photographs relate to two of the three plays in repertory. The first shows Phoebe Waterfield [left], Pamela Dellar [centre] and Norma Shebbeare [right] preparing for the opening night of *Othello*. This photograph captures exactly the sense of last-minute preparation and anxious checking within the dressing room. Norma Shebbeare played the role of Desdemona to Wilfred Harrison's Othello. The costumes for this production were designed by

---

23. Harrison, interview.
24. Cited in a Century Theatre publicity brochure (date unknown).

Promotional photograph of the Century Theatre production of *The Miser* by Molière which opened at Nantwich on 8 July 1953 directed by Abraham Asseo. The costumes and set were designed by John Crockett. From left to right: Pamela Goodwin (later Dellar), Armine Sandford (later Robinson), Leonard Kingston and Norma Shebbeare. From the collections of the Theatre Museum. By courtesy of the Trustees of the Victoria and Albert Museum. Photo: John Dodds.

Osborne Robinson who had produced set and costume designs for early Adelphi productions as far back as 1942, with his designs for the open-air production of Milton's *Comus*. Whilst there is evidence from the photograph of the limited space available within the dressing rooms, they were probably preferable in their newness and cleanliness to many equivalent facilities in the repertory theatres of the period.

The dressing rooms were immediately behind the stage and were the full length and width of one large trailer. As can be seen from John Ridley's design plan for the theatre [on page 128] there were also wash-basins for the actors, two wardrobes and two dressing tables, each seating six actors. The actors could then make their entrances and exits directly on to and off the stage. The overall dimensions of the stage were 19 feet deep by 33 feet wide from wall to wall. The prosecenium opening was 23 feet. The auditorium itself consisted of fifteen rows, each of fifteen seats, constructed on a raked basis.

The second photograph shows a scene in performance from *The Miser* in which the costumes and set were designed by John Crockett. Pamela Goodwin [later Pamela Dellar] is featured on the extreme left of the photograph. Centrestage, Leonard Kingston is flanked [stage right] by Armine Sandford [Robinson] and [stage left] by Norma Shebbeare.

The 'Compass connection' is very evident with Sandford and Goodwin having been Compass actresses and, of course, the set and costumes designed by Crockett. The set design shows Crockett's inventive use of draped materials once again, a technique he perfected in his designs for the Compass Players. The costumes are well conceived in terms of the play's seventeenth-century origins and show an understanding of line and cut. The photograph also shows the relatively modest size of the stage with limited depth and width. When used as part of promotional literature for the company, the photograph was accompanied by the caption 'Let's pretend we're dancing', and the curious eye-lines and posture of the cast indicate an awkward formality and sense of artifice.

A copy of the full list of venues is provided in Appendix D and reveals a circuit that ranged within the north-west Midlands area from Northwich through to Macclesfield: areas which the Adelphis and Compass had been particularly acquainted with. The Century must clearly have supposed that there would be a significant degree of local support in that region. As Ross Wilson had observed, the three plays in repertory broadly represent the three categories under which plays were introduced into the repertory: a reasonably popular crowd-puller, a set text for schools' parties and finally inclusion of a work that would not normally find its way into conventional, commercial repertory. With respect to these broad considerations, the repertory was, I believe, refreshingly catholic, ranging from *The Miser* through to *Mr Bolfry* by Bridie and the relatively experimental and rarely seen work of dramatists such as Marceau and Obey, and Labiche's *Le Voyage de Monsieur Perrichon*. After 1956 and the emergence of new writers such as Osborne and others,

THE CENTURY THEATRE.

BRITAIN'S THEATRE-ON-WHEELS.

A copy of John Ridley's design for the construction of the Century Theatre.

Look Back In Anger was also to feature in the repertory along with Chekhov and Ibsen.

Other plays in the repertory over the early years of the company's existence included Priestley's *I Have Been Here Before*, Eliot's *The Cocktail Party* and Maugham's play *The Sacred Flame*. Whilst Priestley's well-crafted play – with its additionally interesting exploration of the nature of time and human destiny – was an obvious choice for the company, the inclusion of the Maugham play is, perhaps, more problematic. Maugham's plays and the values and culture that informed them are more resonant of the pre-war, commercial West End. Nevertheless, the continuing commercial success of his plays with both regional and London audiences, made the inclusion of his work understandable in terms of balancing the plays of less commercial writers such as Marcel and Ghéon. Generally, there was a reluctance on the part of the London-based newspapers to review a touring theatre like the Century. Theatre in the regions of Britain beyond London, 'north of Watford', was not taken seriously by London-based correspondents. This is most cogently conveyed by the infamous example of this attitude attributed to Bernard Levin. When asked to cover a production in Manchester, Levin is alleged to have protested, "I'm the drama critic, not a foreign correspondent!" One of the Labour government's pieces of legislation that provided some potential support to the new company dated back to the Local Government Act of 1948. Under this Act, local authorities could levy a sixpenny rate per head of population to spend upon the Arts. The aim of this legislation was to stimulate the regional theatres emerging in the post-war years. As I discuss in more detail in my final chapter, because this legislation dealt with only discretionary measures, many local authorities did not feel compelled to act upon it. As Harrison recalls:

> We were pioneers in getting local government to give us a guarantee against loss: the local authorities would provide the site and we persuaded them to give us a guarantee against loss so that if we did not take the money, they would make it up. This was novel – we gave many local authorities the first opportunity they would have to give subsidy to theatre through that means. [25]

Nevertheless, this was the only form of financial subsidy that they received from either local or national authorities.

When the company had applied for Arts Council support as early as 1950 John Ridley remembered that the Council's response had been: 'The Century Theatre is mechanically impossible, artistically impossible, financially impossible and should not be supported.' This assessment carried with it a certain irony in retrospect when, two years later in 1952, the theatre was fully operational and proving to be 'possible'. Nevertheless, the logistics and

---

25. Harrison, correspondence.

cost of keeping the theatre running and its consumption of time and energy
was greater than its founders had anticipated. Furthermore, the theatre was
having to operate artistically and economically in a changing wider climate.
The guiding policy principles of the Arts Council favoured the establishment
of building-based civic theatres in the regions. Whilst the regions had to wait
until 1958 for the building of the Belgrade Theatre in Coventry, nevertheless
this first purpose-built civic theatre had grown out of the successful Arts
Council-funded Midland Theatre Company that had toured from 1946
onwards. Playing at small towns such as Dudley and Nuneaton, providing a
similar service to the Century Theatre, but with it was substantial funding
and without the regular loss of time and energy that the Century faced in
erecting and dismantling their theatre There were other examples of this
kind of trend towards establishing repertory theatres in regional towns and
cities.
   As Rowell states in the following example:

> Interestingly several of them (Guildford in 1946, Ipswich in 1947, Leatherhead in
> 1951) were housed in adapted buildings ... Guildford and Ipswich, for example,
> both started as club-theatres in local halls, Kidderminster (1946), Chesterfield
> (1949), Canterbury (1951) and Leatherhead as cinemas, Derby (1951) as a public
> hall. [26]

Therefore, whilst the Arts Council's refusal to support the company for the
reasons that were given were ungrounded and premature, in the context of
their own policy priorities, their decision was probably justified – if only to
themselves.
   Two years prior to the Century's opening season, Bristol Old Vic were
offering Shakespeare, Molière and a verse drama by Fry. Compared to the
Century's opening season, there is nothing to distinguish between the two
companies' selections. It is a tribute to the companies' combination of energy,
ideals and abilities that, without recourse to State subsidy, they succeeded
in touring a repertory of quality plays to a consistently high artistic standard.
In the sense that many small theatreless towns were enabled to see quality
professional theatre, one recognises the sentiments expressed by a critic from
the *Manchester Evening News*: '"The Century has seemed to a great many
enthusiasts to be the germ of the national theatre of the future".' Whilst I am
clearly not suggesting that this was literally the case, nevertheless the sense
in which the enterprise was built as a result of widespread popular support,
its progressive touring policy and eclectic repertory, the Century project was
characterised by a democratic ideal. In terms of the creation of a national
theatre, Ward had stated as early as 1942: 'The chief danger of a State or
municipal subsidy lay in the measure of control it might entail. The theatre

26. Rowell, pp.81–2.

has always thrived when it has had to face opposition, and overcome obstacles. It will thrive only if the people are made to feel it is their responsibility.' [27] If, therefore, those same sentiments that informed the concept and construction of the Century now seem Quixotic from our more jaded, contemporary perspective, that does not invalidate their egalitarian optimism.

In conclusion, the original Century Theatre company, with obvious changes of personnel, continued to tour from 1952 until 1957. By this time, the theatre needed material overhauling after five years of strenuous touring. Also, there were differing personal and professional interests that necessitated change. After a period in which the Century threatened to fall into disrepair and disuse, an appeal in 1959 led to the theatre going back on tour. In the light of the ferocious independence of the Century's origins, it is ironic that it was the Arts Council and two Independent Television companies that provided most of the financial backing required. Eventually, it made its way to what was, for many years, its final and permanent location in Keswick in the Lake District. At the time of writing, July 2000, a new theatre has been built at Keswick to replace the Blue Box which, after its final season in 1997 – which I had the privilege of attending – was moved to its final placement as part of Snibston Discovery Park, near Hinckley in Leicestershire. There, at what is an exciting educational, technological learning centre, it has resumed 'active service' for both lectures and occasional performances. Supported by Leicestershire Educational and Arts services, it is hoped that the Century may become the centre for a national museum and archive of touring British theatre.

Melvyn Bragg wrote of the Century Theatre:

> There was a special democratic and selfless spirit abroad in the late Forties, and the Century Theatre is a living testament to that: it toured the Midlands and the North in the Fifties and Sixties, plugging gaps left by the decayed ... commercial theatre, seeding interest in the Sixties chain of brick and mortar provincial theatres which would spring up to replace their begetter. [28]

Bragg's summary gives a useful shorthand assessment of the ethos and achievements of the Century Theatre. In its founders' continued commitment to the community, of reaching out to theatreless towns, also to a theatre of integrity contributing to post-war cultural restoration, the Century Theatre remains as a resonant reminder of changing social, cultural and economic fabric. Wilfred Harrison offers a final reflection:

---

27. R H Ward, 'The Art of the Theatre', a speech given at Ilkley, 29 January 1943, the transcript published in the *Ilkley Gazette*.
28. Melvyn Bragg, 'Turn of the Century', *Punch* magazine, 14 September 1983, p.61.

It is because communion between human beings, person with person, is part of the richest human experience that the theatre has a special part to play in human society ... The complete theatre demands the complete actor, the complete person. In the Century Theatre therefore, a member is not engaged simply for his/her talent; his/her person is of significance. [29]

---

29. Wilfred Harrison, 'Century Theatre Policy Statement', 1953. Original document loaned to author by kind permission of Wilfred Harrison, 1990.

6

CONCLUSION

In this, my concluding chapter, I intend to discuss the social, cultural and political conditions of the immediate post-war period and conclude with a summary of the four companies under discussion. In doing so, I shall complete my analysis of the companies in the context of that wider background.

Kenneth Tynan wrote of the great actor-manager, Sir Donald Wolfit:

> In the course of 1944, I saw Wolfit in nearly all the considerable parts in the Shakespearean repertory and out of that surfeit I think I can form an opinion. There has never been an actor of greater gusto than Wolfit; he has dynamism, energy, bulk and stature ... It is grossly unfair, as well as inaccurate, to accuse him of being a 'ham'; if 'ham' means what I take it to mean, one who rants and roars and strikes poses ... Wolfit's error lies in cherishing what I can only describe as a provincial inferiority complex to the extent of being unable or unwilling to work for anyone but himself. If he can overcome that, the West End will acquire an actor of greater technical power than it currently possesses. [1]

I quote from Tynan's assessment of Wolfit because both the actor and critic represent significant aspects of important reference points and trends within post-war British theatre, and our critical definition and reception of its output. Tynan's, perhaps, was the leading and most articulate voice to interrogate the condition of post-war British theatre. In doing so, he wrote several celebrated critiques of the verse drama movement whilst bemoaning the essentially parochial, bourgeois nature of the English stage and its principal dramatists.

It was Tynan who campaigned for a revitalised theatre which would necessitate new writers, and who championed Osborne's *Look Back in Anger*. Tynan also, of course, went on to become Literary Advisor for the long-awaited National Theatre. Wolfit, meanwhile, represented the last of the great actor-managers whose traditions went back to the nineteenth-century precedents such as Kean and Beerbohm-Tree. Actors and actresses such as Wilfred Harrison and Nina Evans had learnt some of their trade through working with Wolfit's touring company. Effectively, the actor-managers had enjoyed their final period of sustained influence in the pre-1914 period. By the middle of the century, the economics of touring such companies proved

---

1.   Kenneth Tynan, *A View of the English Stage 1944–63* (Davis/Poynter, 1975), pp.23–4.

increasingly difficult, and the acting style associated with them seemed dated and inappropriate to many. Nevertheless, Wolfit had won many admirers and enjoyed great popularity for his recitals of Shakespeare in London during the height of the Blitz. However, with the ensuing demise of Wolfit and that tradition, one can also recognise the growing demand for a new kind of theatre with its own agenda and practitioners in the years following on from the end of the war. It should be remembered that Ward and Harrison, amongst others, made their own contribution to that debate.

Andrew Davies writes in his *Other Theatres* that:

> The Second World War provided a tremendous boost for non-commercial drama, especially when it is born in mind that a League of Audiences survey of 1939 revealed that 92% of the British people had never been to the theatre. Many of the assumptions and conventions supported by the West End theatre – the barrier between amateur and professional and performer and spectator, the select audiences, the formalised settings, the emphasis on expensive production values, the subject-matter of plays – had been challenged and weakened. For the first time since the Elizabethans, this country possessed what was virtually a national drama. [2]

This state of affairs within the non-commercial theatre movement in 1945 reflected a growing trend that had gained momentum through the war years with the work of companies such as the Pilgrims, Adelphis and Compass Players. The Unity Theatre was able to report upon an increased membership of nearly 7,000, whilst the Merseyside Unity had also taken the step of expanding into new premises in 1944. The Co-operative Society had formed a National Association of Drama Associations, whilst the British Drama League announced in 1945 that 500 amateur dramatic societies were affiliated to its organisation. This substantial and remarkable increase in the popular interest and involvement in the arts, frequently with leftist ideological dimensions, reflects in its own way the idealism and expectation for significant social and political change within Britain by 1945. The return of a Labour government in 1945 with one of the largest majorities in parliamentary history is well documented. There were 393 Labour MPs returned whilst the Communist Party had two representatives in Willie Gallacher in West Fife and Phil Piratin in Mile End. In the first session of that Parliament, the Government benches rang to a rendition of 'The Red Flag'. However, if all of this evidence suggests a society on the brink of radical revolution, as some on the right wing of the Conservative Party feared, then the truth was depressingly different. Clement Attlee had appointed a Cabinet who represented experience rather than revolutionary socialism. The social and economic problems that faced the country were immense after six years of war. The widespread social concern and unrest at the failure of the pre-war

---

2.   Andrew Davies, *Other Theatres* (Macmillan, 1987), p.136,

Government to effectively tackle the injustices of poor housing, inadequate schooling and health care for the working-classes had been fuelled through the war years.

Wartime conditions of austerity and shortages, the breaking down of conventional social and economic roles with many women working in heavy industries such as armaments, and the creation of a common ideological consensus against Fascism contributed powerfully to the conviction amongst the majority of people that significant social change must follow on from the ending of the war in 1945. Plans towards this post-war social and economic transformation were already being made as early as 1942 with the publication of the Beveridge Report:

> The war appeared to demonstrate the efficacy of taking work to the workers and of industrial diversification. The Uthwatt and Scott Reports dealt specifically with urban and rural problems ... The development of New Towns was envisaged. But of most interest to the public was the Beveridge Report, with its proposals for a far-reaching and universal scheme of social insurance ... Mass Observation reported in its November 1942 *Bulletin* that many people expected the war to be followed by a return to mass unemployment and less money. Beveridge affirmed the need for a successful battle against the five 'giants' of want, disease, ignorance, squalor and idleness ... An 85 per cent poll was recorded in its favour. [3]

Along with the eventual implementation of the Report's principal recommendations in 1948 came the Butler Education Act of 1944, which promised increased educational provision and opportunities for all children, particularly for those from disadvantaged, working-class backgrounds.

The Beveridge Report and the Butler Act did of course represent important and substantial social and economic legislation. Nevertheless, it would be wrong and simplistic to assume that they necessarily delivered what many ordinary people and social reformers of the Left expected and had campaigned for.

It is neither appropriate nor within my remit to attempt a detailed political or economic analysis within the context of this short concluding chapter. Nevertheless, I do think that it is important to recognise the changing nature of British society and some of the progressive legislation that was introduced by the Labour government. Theatre as a cultural activity and product clearly does not function or develop in a vacuum, separated from its wider social and cultural context. In the light of the ideological idealism and broadly progressive aims that motivated and characterised all four companies, their hopes for a renewed theatre that would be part of a transformed society mirror, perhaps, the wider hopes and mood of society at that time. Equally, the disappointments and difficulties that they eventually faced, particularly

---

3.   C J Bartlett, *A History of Post-War Britain 1945–74* (Longman, 1977), p.8.

in the case of the Adelphi Guild, the Compass and the Century Theatre, reflected not only internal company disputes but also, I believe, the increasingly changing societal context in which they endeavoured to exist and survive. This societal context encompassed the diminishing of the popular, broad left front and also the changes in British theatre and its location and funding in the post-war period.

With Britain becoming increasingly dependent on American aid, the signs of the ending of Empire with the independence awarded to India in 1947, and the emergence of the Cold War ideological climate, the mood in British society became increasingly depressed. Shortages inevitably continued after 1945, with rationing remaining until 1956. With the common battle against Fascism apparently won, progressive legislation passed, yet with the growing impatience amongst the public with the Labour government of whom so much was expected, support for the political and cultural initiatives of the broad left began to be undermined.

With the apparent failure of the Labour government to deal with the aggravated issue of shortages caused by the severe winters of 1947 and 1948 and the spectre of rising unemployment, the Government was forced to announce a General Election in 1950. Labour were returned but with a much reduced majority: 315 seats to the Conservatives. Significantly, the Communists lost the two seats they had gained in 1945. However, whilst the Government survived in the short term, the divisions within the Party grew between those who sought to reaffirm Socialist policies and values in key areas such as the social programme, and others whose main aim was to present a Government who were reliable in power and pursuing moderate, centre-right policies. Fenner Brockway, the socialist and pacifist who had founded the No-Conscription Fellowship, criticised the Government for its spending on Defence and the absence of any progressive social programme in his *Outside the Right*. Also, Richard Crossman in his *New Fabian Essays* criticised Attlee and his Cabinet for having no definable theoretical basis on which to plan further reform. Within twelve months of their narrow victory the Labour government were obliged to go to the country once more. The remnants of popular support had significantly ebbed and in October 1951 a Conservative administration was elected. However their success reflected as much a widespread disgruntlement with continuing shortages and austerity measures, brought to a head finally by what was seen by Government critics as the wasteful expenditure on the Festival of Britain in 1951. Bartlett summarises the attitude of the Conservative Party at this time:

> Conservative elation at their victory was tempered by the daunting economic situation. Harold Macmillan commented on 28 October [1951]: 'It is 1940 without bombing and casualties – but also without the sense of national unity.' ... The new government faced rising prices and unemployment and a difficult time abroad. [4]

---

4.   Ibid, p.49.

The Conservatives had not so much won an election in terms of their policies and manifesto. The election result indicated a disillusioned mood amongst the people. After the apparent failure of the Labour government to implement the changes expected following the optimism of 1945, there was invariably a reactionary return to the Conservative political establishment for practical, not ideological reasons. Within this climate of the politics of pragmatism, it was not surprising that organisations and companies such as the PPU and Unity Theatre became increasingly marginalised. There was also an ongoing debate in both which questioned the political and ethical basis on which their work was to continue. In an interesting parallel with the circumstances that led to the demise of the Adelphi Guild, internal disputes and politics within the London Unity resulted in its near collapse in the years immediately following the war. A faction led by the influential Ted Willis sought to break away from the company's amateur status and establish a professional company. Colin Chambers has discussed this matter in considerable detail in his exhaustive study *The Story of the Unity Theatre*, from which I quote:

> Unity's leadership under Ted Willis was enthused with the nation's optimism and issued bold statements of intent ... the establishment of a professional company, which earlier in Unity's history had only been thwarted by the outbreak of war ... Willis pushed through its establishment against bitter opposition ... [After the eventual collapse of the enterprise ...] Willis later admitted the artistic failure and economic madness of the project but maintained, with some justification, that the idea behind it was correct. For him it proved, sadly, that Unity's strength could only lie in the achievements of small-scale political work based on limited resources, but he believed still that the time for such activities had passed. [5]

The severe blow that the failure of the Unity Repertory Company made to the rest of the Unity movement should not be underestimated. Many within Unity accused Willis and others of acting purely on the basis of personal and professional ambition, and argued that the attempt to run the company on a professional, commercial basis would inevitably dilute its political function and repertory. Nevertheless, in the light of the Arts Council's policy commitment towards – to use its own phrase – 'few, but roses', and its swing away from CEMA's wartime criteria of supporting the touring of theatreless communities, Willis may have been endeavouring to respond to that policy change in a way that might have offered Unity the financial subsidy and continuity that it needed.

As far as the fortunes of the PPU were concerned, with the ending of the war came a fall in membership. Nevertheless with the horrific bombing of Hiroshima and Nagasaki in 1945 and the plight of many thousands of refugees across Europe after the war, there were many issues and causes that the PPU could – and did – commit itself to. The movement also continued to devote

---

5.   Colin Chambers, *The Story of Unity Theatre* (Lawrence and Wishart, 1969), pp.264–78.

financial support to research into non-violent resistance and out of this came a project known as Operation Gandhi. This was a series of planned anti-atomic demonstrations and led to a sit-down outside the War Office on 11 January 1952 and the start of many demonstrations at the Aldermaston Atomic Weapons Research Establishment in April of the same year. From 1958 onwards, the first of the famous Aldermaston Marches began from the same site. Out of the relative success of Operation Gandi came the formation of the Direct Action Committee Against Nuclear War which eventually merged with the Committee of 100 [which had originated the CND in 1958] in 1961. Therefore, whilst actual membership of the PPU fell in the decade following the war, its activities continued and diversified.

Towards the end of the following decade, in November 1969, Richard Ward attended a Prisoners for Peace march and read some of his poetry in the crypt of what had been Dick Shepherd's church, St Martin-in-the-Fields. It was his last public activity before his death one month later.

CEMA, under the chairmanship of Maynard Keynes, had possessed a liberal and broadly progressive character. Keynes had helped initiate what was effectively the first State involvement in theatre management and ownership, when personally authorising the purchase of the Bristol Old Vic in 1943 in order to ensure its survival. This was followed by the establishing of a repertory theatre and touring circuit at Salisbury, the Midland Theatre Company based at Coventry Technical College, and the unsuccessful Swansea Repertory. Under his leadership CEMA was able to prove a benificent supporter of small, non-commercial companies such as the Adelphis. However, with the ending of the war the newly-formed Arts Council came to be seen increasingly as acting in the mainstream interests of the cultural establishment, a charge it has continued to face periodically through to the writing of this book. In the 1948-49 period, the Arts Council allocated a quarter of its entire budget to opera at Covent Garden, the plans for the eagerly awaited regional community arts centres were deferred, and the Drama Panel was effectively controlled by representatives from the West End establishment. From having, as CEMA, at least the potential of facilitating progressive, non-commercial theatre, as the Arts Council, it appeared to have become a financial supporter of the established commercial sector. Also, despite its stated commitment to develop regional theatre, much of its money and attention was diverted to London.

With the commercial theatrical establishment based in London and with its direct, almost exclusive, control over touring commercial repertory, a suffocating monopoly overshadowed much of British theatre. Writing in 1946, Norman Marshall observed that, with the ending of the war:

> Theatres were sold and resold at prices so inflated that none of the managements would buy ... For instance, a theatre which before the war had difficulty in getting a tenant at a rent of £50 per week ... a few months ago demanded, and got, a

minimum rental of £600 a week plus a percentage over a certain figure. To make matters worse, the theatre is mainly controlled by a small group of managements. At present, there are only sixteen straight plays to be seen in the centre of London, if one excludes two farces from the list. One management is responsible for eight of these sixteen plays. [6]

The principal West End management that Marshall refers to was euphemistically called 'The Group', which was in fact directly owned by the impresario Prince Littler. By the late 1940s Littler controlled nearly half of the surviving West End theatres and over 70 per cent of the main regional touring venues. With two other impresarios, Frank Fortesque and Harry Hanson, controlling the touring repertory circuit through their respective companies, this constricting financial power base resulted in a commercial West End system centred upon 'stars', in plays that offered a pleasing, if illusory, anaesthetic to the austerity of the times. Of course, there were fine productions including Martin Browne's season at the Mercury and, more notably, his production of the premiere of Eliot's *The Cocktail Party* at the inaugural Edinburgh Festival of 1947 starring Alec Guinness.

Christopher Fry continued to enjoy success with his verse dramas and at Stratford, the young Peter Brook achieved critical acclaim for his production of *Love's Labour's Lost*. From the continent, the work of Sartre, Anouilh and Barrault were all critically acclaimed. Performers such as Olivier, Gielgud, Richardson, Redgrave, Jack Hawkins, Ashcroft and Thorndike all gave outstanding and memorable performances during this period. Nevertheless the British theatre seemed caught once more in the depressingly familiar territory of middle-class audiences supporting what was almost exclusively an unchallenging, bourgeois cultural activity. This cultural exclusivity was at critical odds with the major social and political changes characterising not only post-war Britain but the world. With the collapse of the British Empire and with Europe increasingly dominated by the ideological polarities of the capitalist USA and Stalinist USSR, the absence of new writers and plays to explore and reflect this world seemed untenable to critics such as Tynan. As Hinchliffe observes:

> Around 1950 verse drama looked like the only living thing in the British theatre ... it was spoken by such great performers as Olivier, Gielgud, Alec Guinness, Rex Harrison ... It met the post-war desire for colour, fancy and escape ... *Murder in the Cathedral* was, in context, very successful but the context was not the world in which his [Eliot's] audience lived and to which they returned at the end of the play. And Canterbury Cathedral was not the commercial theatre; it had a congregation rather than an audience. [7]

---

6. Norman Marshall, *The Other Theatre* (John Lehmann, 1947), p.226.
7. Arnold Hinchliffe, *British Theatre 1950–70* (Blackwell, 1974), p.33.

As interesting as they are in their elegant and sophisticated handling of ideas and language, Eliot's and Fry's plays inhabit expressly an insular and reactionary ideological climate. The theoretical and fictive world constructed by Eliot is informed by a reactionary, Anglo-Catholic conservatism. In his *Notes Towards the Definition of Culture* [1948], Eliot built upon his social criticism of the pre-war period and effectively advocated the formation of a 'Christian culture' as the only alternative to what he perceived as a threatening, egalitarian secularisation of society. Tynan took Eliot to task in his article 'Prose and the Playwright' published in 1954:

> One of the handicaps of poetry is that penumbra of holiness, the legacy of the nineteenth century ... tolerating sentimental excesses we could never forgive in prose: ... 'What devil left the door on the latch for these doubts to enter? And then you came back, you the angel of destruction – just as I felt sure. In a moment, at your touch, there is nothing but ruin.' Exit, you might expect into a snowstorm, but you would be wrong. The lines come not from Victorian melodrama but from *The Cocktail Party*, printed as prose. [8]

It was not until the breakthrough that George Devine succeeded in achieving with his English Stage Company at the Royal Court, and other developments such as the building and opening of the first new regional theatre since the war, the Belgrade at Coventry in 1958, that the circumstances began to emerge where new writing in theatres might be given a proper opportunity. Of course, these developments, whilst much sought after and needed, did not automatically happen and neither were their achievements without difficulties or their critics. However, what initiatives such as the Royal Court, the Belgrade and Littlewood's Theatre Workshop did signify in their different ways, was an increased responsiveness to the social, cultural and political changes happening around them.

   Against the nullifying background of the commercially-dominated West End, such initiatives offered a sense of hope and opposition. Within regional repertory theatres, there had also been initiatives such as the establishment of CORT – the Confederation of Repertory Theatres – in 1944, which became the Conference of Repertory Theatres in 1950. This in itself reflected a commitment to the mutual support of non-commercial repertory theatre outside London. In February 1948 there had been an important Theatre Conference held in London and chaired by J B Priestley who in 1947 had published a pamphlet entitled *The Arts Under Socialism*. The West End theatre managements boycotted the conference and there was also a disappointing failure on behalf of trade union representatives to attend. Nevertheless, the event does seem to have activated the government. The level of Entertainments Tax on live theatre was halved and removed altogether from small rural populations. The National Theatre Act was passed in 1949

---

8.   Tynan, p.143.

although this was to remain nominally symbolic for a number of years to come. The Local Government Act of 1948, which I referred to in my previous chapter, did give Local Authorities the opportunity of making a discretionary 6d annual rate on entertainments. However, few chose to do so, and it remains a matter of frustrating speculation as to the effect that a mandatory clause might have had in terms of regional developments of the arts. In all of this, both within the capital and in the rest of the country, the extent to which theatre was liberated out of its predominantly bourgeois insularity is open to question. In *A Good Night Out*, John McGrath questions whether the Royal Court ever substantially altered the theatre-going habits of the middle-classes and their hold on theatre as a cultural activity. There is no evidence that large numbers of working-class audiences were motivated into attending theatre during this period, or indeed, subsequently.

Similarly, the socialist values and aims that motivated Littlewood to found a popular 'People's Theatre' in London's East End was to end acrimoniously with the Theatre Royal at Stratford East becoming as much an 'off-West End' venue for established audiences as much as a service to its immediate, working-class communities. The financial pressure on productions to transfer into the capital's commercial venues, along with internal divisions within the company, led to Littlewood leaving Stratford East, and the professional theatre, for good. Nevertheless, even with these critical reservations, some definable progress had been made within the scope that the British theatre offered new writers. As Hinchliffe again observes:

> 'Before 1956', to quote Tynan, 'it was necessary – if one were to be eligible for dramatic treatment – to have an annual income of more than £3,000 net or be murdered in the house of someone who had.' [9]

One major social and cultural trend that I have yet to mention, and that was clearly of great importance in terms of both theatre-going and popular culture generally, was the increasing availability and influence of television. Prior to the war, the advent of 'the talkies' had made the cinema hugely popular, reinforced by cheap admission prices and, in the bigger auditoriums, a warm and comfortable environment. The cinema had faced criticism from many on the Left during the inter-war years – including Ward – mainly because of its associations with the exploitative commercial interests of the Hollywood film industry. More practically, it offered an attractive and inexpensive alternative to the commercial repertory theatres and was therefore a significant threat to business. After the war, television began to assume the same threat to the theatre that the cinema had in the nineteen-thirties.

Television drama began transmission in 1946, although it was with the opening of Independent – commercial – Television in 1955 that television

---

9.   Hinchliffe, p.45.

began to assert a more prevalent and lasting influence. It was the provincial commercial theatre that took the hardest blow. From the mid to the late nineteen-fifties, television sets became affordable to many and the medium quickly developed as a principal source of popular entertainment. However, its advent, in many respects, was not as entirely negative or catastrophic as many in both the theatre and on the Left initially feared. Whilst many commercial repertory theatre companies undoubtedly did go out of business, one should not necessarily sentimentalise their loss. Positively, writers on the broad Left such as John McGrath, Trevor Griffiths, Alan Plater, Dennis Potter and many others began, and continued, to write for television, understanding its potency as popular culture for the debate of ideas and issues with the mass of the population. Also, it may be argued that early serials such as *Coronation Street* and *Z Cars* found their social-realist style and momentum through the breakthrough afforded in theatre by writers who responded to the crisis that television threatened:

> The provision of food as an adjunct (or often alternative) to the hasty interval drink in the bar; the opening of the theatre during the day with coffee and culture in the form of exhibitions, talks and club activities as an additional attraction ... and the inauguration in 1958 ... of a training scheme for theatre administrators. [10]

Theatres of Conscience: A Final Reflection

In this final section of my concluding chapter I intend to summarise the principal issues that have arisen from my study of the four companies. In doing so, I shall be attempting to place them within the context of the wider developments of which they were a small, but significant, part.

The Pilgrim Players represented an early attempt during wartime Britain to take professional theatre to theatre-less communities suffering the endemic deprivations of those times. Their choice of plays for their repertory reflected those particular beliefs and values of Martin Browne and his wife Henzie Raeburn. Consequently there was an unmistakable emphasis upon an essentially conventional understanding of religious drama. This ideological dimension to their work, whilst most certainly not shared by all company members, was reinforced through Browne's own close personal and professional relationship with T S Eliot. Browne's wider reputation was inextricably bound up with his success as the director of Eliot's plays. With his short, but successful, 1946 Mercury season of Plays by Poets, and his 1947 production of *The Cocktail Party* at Edinburgh, Browne was closely affiliated to what appeared to represent the main way forward for British play writing after 1945. However, critics such as Tynan and Hinchliffe –

---

10. George Rowell and Anthony Jackson, *The Repertory Movement* (Cambridge University Press, 1984), p.87.

amongst others – challenged the appropriateness of verse as a theatrical language, and also the insular conservatism that characterised much of its output. Through the continuing secularisation of society and the challenging of orthodox, conservative theology by liberals such as Dietrich Bonhoeffer and those, like Bishop John Robinson, influenced by Bonhoeffer's writings, the concept and function of religious drama seemed increasingly remote from the social, cultural and political changes taking place in that period.

During this post-war period, there has been a continuing fall in church attendances whilst organisations like RADIUS have seen their membership decline dramatically. As Hinchliffe asserts:

> Today we lack that shared morality on which tragedy rested. We ask questions; indeed, Brechtian theatre obliges us to ask questions. The Elizabethans would never have thought of asking whether or not Romeo and Juliet died a worthless death but we wonder whether Celia [a central character from *The Cocktail Party* who dies a martyr's death] could not have sacrificed herself less wastefully. [11]

Richard Heron Ward represents a more radical and non-conformist approach to theatre and also to the analysis of social and political issues. This in itself reflects his wider ideological and ethical concerns: for example, his involvement with both the ILP and the PPU. His close contact and friendship with both Canon Dick Shepherd and Max Plowman helps to identify the core of his thinking within that framework of liberal, ethical socialism. In his writings for *Peace News* prior to the war and his manifesto article 'Theatre of Persons', we discover an individual of immense energy and passion who sought to combine his ideals with the practical requirements of touring theatre under difficult circumstances. In the post-war period, in addition to helping to form the Century Theatre, he also achieved some recognition through two particular books, both published by Gollancz. One, *Gallery of Mirrors*, is an autobiographical reflection upon his life, whilst *A Drug Taker's Notes* is an account of his experiments with LSD. His experiments and account of that hallucinogenic drug preceded Huxley's better-known *Doors of Perception*. In terms of his theatre work with the Adelphi Players, he wrote in 1947:

> I think we did begin to discover new ways of writing, producing and acting plays, rather as if we began to peel away the old theatre, much of it corrupt and deathly, and caught sight of a new one underneath. Whether we managed to put across that new theatre is another matter, and whether anyone, moved by our example, will follow us, is also another matter. But one or two things are certain; there is a vast potential audience for intelligent plays which have something to say to human persons, and there is a vast need for new ways of saying it. [12]

---

11. Hinchliffe, p.44.
12. R H Ward, 'The Adelphi Players: A Tabloid History', *Peace News*, 29 August 1947, p.5.

In imagining that a play such as *Holy Family* might indicate the form that new writing would take after the war, Ward was mistaken whilst sharing the predominant view of the time. However, his impassioned denunciation of the reactionary commercial theatre establishment, and his deeply-held conviction in the aesthetic and educative potential within theatre, place him in that tradition of pioneers who, from Granville-Barker onwards, sought to establish an 'alternative' theatre of integrity and imagination.

John Crockett's work with the Compass Players is characterised by a similar commitment to take imaginative and distinctive theatre to areas and communities which had previously remained outside of the existing touring circuits. The company's output was distinguished by Crockett's highly developed visual aesthetic, resulting on experimentations with dance, masks, music and mime-productions such as *The Quest* and *Dr Faustus* expressed this work at its most innovative. Their attempts to launch an early example of Theatre in Education also deserve wider recognition.

Finally, the Century Theatre represented a unique attempt to create a touring theatre and travelling company which, in providing a fully equipped venue, would overcome the difficulties of constantly playing in varied, non-standard venues. In its own special way, it reflects and embodies the optimism and idealism of the immediate post-war years more than any of the other companies.

Whilst it was necessarily run more on a relatively commercial basis than the other three companies, its founders, Ward, Wilfred Harrison and John Ridley, still sought to implement the ethos of 'The Theatre of Persons.' Its initial demise as a touring theatre was the result of two different but complementary factors. Firstly, there were differences of opinion within the company as to its aims and the extent to which different factions within the company perceived their own professional interests. Secondly, there was the broader social, cultural and economic climate in which even more conventional touring companies were being overlooked by the Arts Council, in favour of the establishment of building-based regional theatres and an orientation towards the centre and the subsidised and commercial London concerns. Add to that the continuing shortage of basic resources such as petrol in the decade after war and it is not difficult, with hindsight, to predict the problems that the Century would face. Nevertheless, as if embodying the tenacious integrity and commitment of its founders, the 'Blue Box' has survived to a dignified and appropriate semi-retirement at Snibsworth Discovery Park, providing an educational and creative facility into the new millennium.

So much has happened in British theatre over the last fifty years, much of it encouraging in its ideological and cultural diversity. It is true that the commercial theatre, still essentially London-based, can seem as depressingly reactionary and complacent as its nineteen-thirties counterpart. Ward and others believed that it could not survive the war; but, despite pressure from the cinema and television, it has proved enduring if not endearing. David Lister, in a 1993 article for *The Independent*, discussed the decline in theatre for, especially, for the younger generation:

> Later this week [mid-December 1993] the Arts Council is expected to shift funds away from some of the country's best-known theatres to contemporary dance and the visual arts, on the grounds that these are art forms whose audiences are expanding. The theatre is getting the cold shoulder and not only in terms of funding ... It is now nearly fifty years since the end of the war. Why has theatre ceased to be a touchstone of popular culture? [13]

Along with Andrew Davies in his commendable overview of alternative British theatre in the twentieth century, *Other Theatres*, I retain strong reservations about the issue of whether theatre has ever been a 'touchstone of popular culture'. I fully agree with the following assertions that Davies makes:

> The limited role that theatre plays in most people's everyday lives: not since the early sixteenth-century has more than a fraction of the country ever attended live theatre ... Alternative theatre in Britain has never dented this state of affairs, resulting in, for instance, the perennial complaints about the lack of new plays or writers. The Labour movement has been of little or no help, and the attempt to introduce theatre into schools is being undermined by lack of funds. [14]

It would be wrong, of course, to sentimentalise the aims, ideals and work of the four companies that I have examined. Equally, I have endeavoured to be scrupulously objective in evaluating their significance and achievements. Nevertheless, in the context of their common understanding of theatre as something which was of inherent value to persons and communities, they embodied a commitment of unswerving integrity and purpose. Whilst none of the companies ever produced important new writers, ground-breaking productions or outstanding individuals, it was never really within either their capacity or intention to do so.

What they did achieve, I believe, was to maintain remarkably high standards of performance in terms of their limited resources, personnel and the ever-changing demands that non-standard venues made upon touring theatre. In their choice of repertory and their commitment to an egalitarian, community company existence, they pre-empted significant developments within oppositional, post-war theatre. Ultimately, in their breaking of new ground in terms of the venues and audiences they played to, I would argue that they helped to create the social and cultural conditions which facilitated the eventual growth of regional and community theatre after 1945.

---

13. David Lister, 'A nation suffering from stage fright', *The Independent*, 14 December 1993.
14. Davies, p.208.

In conclusion, for many people in wartime Britain and in the decade immediately following, these four companies provided them with entertainment, recreation and the stimulus that only good theatre, with its imagination, debate and artistry, can provide. If a manifesto article such as Ward's 'Theatre of Persons' now seems improbably optimistic and principled in its espousal of a relationship between theatre and society, this may remind us uncomfortably of the jaundiced pragmatism and compromise of our contemporary political and cultural climate.

For me, researching these four companies over quite a long period of time has stimulated and reaffirmed some of my own values, aims and concerns as both a researcher and playwright.

My growing awareness of writers and practitioners such as Richard Ward and John Crockett, and their attempts to formulate and implement a creative, left-field understanding of society and the arts, has strengthened my own resolve within that ongoing project and debate. The friendships that I have made with a wide variety of former actors, directors and writers – especially Wilfred Harrison, Cecil Davies and Pamela Dellar – have proved stimulating and enriching.

I will conclude with two final quotations, one from the writer Edward Blishen, himself a conscientious objector, the other from Ward. For me, these quotations exemplify the humane values and tenacious, if precarious, sense of optimism that characterised those 'Theatres of Conscience':

> The RAF bombed two great dams in the Ruhr. Reporting that 4,000 people had drowned, and 120,000 made homeless, the *Evening Standard* described the event as 'majestic'. I wondered what the German adjective had been for the bombing of Coventry ... [15]

> The public, albeit unconsciously, is looking for a Reformation in the theatre. Sooner or later, it will get it. [16]

---

15. Edward Blishen, *A Cack-handed War* (Thames and Hudson, 1972), pp.155–57.
16. Ward, p.5.

Appendix A

List of Company Contributors from the Pilgrim, Adelphi and Compass Players and the Century Theatre

The following persons – some, at at time of printing, now sadly deceased – all provided invaluable assistance in the preparation of research material for this book, through interviews, correspondence, and the loan of out-of-print books and articles and other various kinds of unique, primary source material. Their names are given in alphabetical order.

Audrey Browne
Margot van der Burgh
John Byrom
Anne Crockett
Cecil and Marion Davies
Maurice Daniels
Pam Dellar
Nina Evans
Collin Hanson
Wilfred and Peggy Harrison
Bettina and John Headley
Bill Hetherington, Archivist at the Peace Pledge Union.
Martin Heller
George Ineson
Pamela Keily
Canon Philip Lamb
Henry Livings
Raymond Parkes
Greta Plowman
Armine and Norman 'Rob' Robinson.
Molly Sole
Norman Tyrell
Arthur Ross Wilson

Appendix B

Cecil Davies, the *Daily Express*, and Conscientious Objectors

As briefly mentioned in Chapter 3, Cecil Davies was the victim of a malicious 'sting' by the *Daily Express* just prior to the outbreak of war, in an article headlined 'Conchie No.1'. This article, and the malign, reactionary ideas that informed it, offers a disturbing indication of the latent hostility, in some quarters, to objectors at this time.

The following short quotation comes from an account of this experience that Cecil Davies gave to Felicity Goodal who cites it in her informative book *A Question of Conscience – Conscientious Objection in the Two World Wars* (Sutton Publishing, 1997) p.89:

> When conscription was introduced and the first lot of conscripts were to register, a reporter of the *Daily Express* went to a meeting at University College [where Davies was a nineteen-year-old student] in order to buttonhole a potential CO, and they got a friend of mine called Harold Thomson. And then they discovered that he was a year older and wouldn't be in the first wave as it were, so they said, 'Haven't you got a friend?' So he rang me up and said ... would I take it on, so I said yes, to publicise the cause. They came to see me, took that appalling photo – I didn't realise it was appalling at the time – they'd really stood me up in order that people would say I was a lounge lizard and all the rest of it.

> The photograph [of Davies posing in debonair fashion in front of a mantelpiece] ... was taken in Fleet Street somewhere, in their offices. They took me out to a pub, gave me some drinks and I suppose I was a bit naive and I think all the things I said were things I meant in that period. It came out the next day and they ran it a second day as well, as an inside story.

The article and photograph brought Cecil Davies a rather unpleasant 'celebrity' status, with an unscrupulous freelance journalist trying, unsuccessfully, to exploit the article with a proposal that Davies be photographed receiving a white feather from a society woman.

Davies desperately sought anonymity and went to stay with a friend, venturing out only with the aid of a hat and dark glasses. He remembers that:

> I had a terrible post bag, a few supporters, but on the whole pretty awful shit – literally in some cases ... It wasn't very pleasant. However, I didn't regret it, I suppose if I regretted anything it was how I had been conned over the photo.

Appendix C

The Second Company of the Adelphi Players' Summary Syllabus for Work in Schools, Summer 1946

IN ASSOCIATION WITH THE ARTS COUNCIL

THE SECOND COMPANY OF

THE ADELPHI PLAYERS

President : DAME SYBIL THORNDIKE

Direction : R. H. WARD

ALL COMMUNICATIONS TO THE GENERAL SECRETARY,
38, ABBEY ROAD, LONDON, N.W.8.
Tel : MAIda Vale 2675.

Dear

In the course of our work during the last four or five
years, work often involving performances for young people who
have not long left school, we have been made aware of the
eagerness of the majority of them for a proper understanding
of the place of the Theatre in the lives of ordinary men and
women.   The theatre can afford an insight into human life and
experience of which a generation faced with the task of
re-making a civilisation stands in absolute need. But young
people will feel little interest in it unless they understand
both its significance for themselves and 'how it works' in
practical terms. They need to be encouraged not only to visit
the theatre and to make healthy criticism of it when they do
so, but also to act and produce their own plays themselves.

We know that in a great many schools much is done to give
the children a knowledge of the drama and of their country's
dramatic heritage. Such schools may or may not feel that they
need to avail themselves of the scheme outlined below. But we
know, too, that many schools are understaffed and that those
staff-members who would like to treat the subject more fully
are often prevented by circumstances from doing so.

Meanwhile there is a danger that many of the generation
just growing up will enter upon their adult lives with little
or no knowledge of the theatre, whether in its sociological
or its artistic aspects. It seems to us that this is a condition of affairs which should be mitigated wherever possible—
especially at a time when the Government, through the Arts
Council, is recognising the theatre as a necessary part of our
national life.

Attached to this letter you will find the syllabus of a
scheme which this company proposes to carry out, in conjunc-

[P.T.O.

tion with Local Education Authorities, during the Summer term
of 1946; also attached is an explanation of the methods by
which the syllabus will be carried out by five members of the
company, two of them trained teachers as well as experienced
actors.   A fee of 20 guineas is asked for each day's work in
a school.

An Advisory Committee has been set up to assist The
Adelphi Players, those who serve on it being Bernard de
Bunsen, Esq., J. T. Hill, Esq., A.C.I.S., A.L.A.A. (Chief
Education Officer, Ipswich), Miss H. J. Wood, M.A. (Headmistress, Basingstoke High School) as well as certain members
of the Company. The enclosed syllabus and its amplification
have been approved by the Committee.

If, as a Chief Education Officer or an individual
Headmistress or Headmaster, you would like to avail yourself
of The Adelphi Players' services under this scheme, please be
kind enough to communicate as soon as possible with The
General Secretary, The Adelphi Players, 38, Abbey Road,
London, N.W.8. Our Tours Manager, Miss Elisabeth Fletcher,
will make arrangements to call on you if required.   Enquiries
will be dealt with in rotation. Late applicants may therefore
find their choice of dates limited. It will be helpful if
Chief Education Officers will state the number of days on
which the Players can be used in their area. In the case of
individual Headmistresses or Headmasters it will be taken for
granted, unless otherwise stated, that only one day's work
will be required.

Yours truly,

Director.

THE SECOND COMPANY OF

THE ADELPHI PLAYERS

38, ABBEY ROAD, LONDON, N.W.8

President : Dame Sybil Thorndike　　　　　　　*Director :* R. H. Ward
General Secretary : M. S. Sole　　*Tours Manager :* Elisabeth Fletcher, B.A. (Econ.) Leeds

DEMONSTRATION WORK IN SCHOOLS

SUMMER, 1946

Advisory Committee :

Bernard De Bunsen, Esq.

J. T. Hill, Esq., A.C.I.S., A.L.A.A.,
　Chief Education Officer, Ipswich.

Miss H. J. Wood, B.A.,
　Headmistress, Basingstoke High School.

Cecil W. Davies, Esq., B.A., Lond.,
　The Adelphi Players.

Wilfred Harrison, Esq., B.Sc., Sheffield,
　The Adelphi Players.

Miss M. S. Sole,
　The Adelphi Players (Secretary to the Committee).

SYLLABUS

GENERAL AIM

To stimulate interest in stage plays, and to encourage an appreciation of their acting,
production and purpose.

(1) **Class Work :** (Class—maximum 40.　Age 14 plus.)
　　　　　　　　(Time 80-90 minutes.)

　　AIM :　　　To show how the acted play is developed from the written play.

　　Matter :　　　　(i) The written word.
　　　　　　　　　　(ii) Speech.
　　　　　　　　　　(iii) Movement.
　　　　　　　　　　(iv) Character.
　　　　　　　　　　(v) Plot.
　　　　　　　　　　(vi) Production.
　　　　　　　　　　(vii) The finished play—its place in human life.

(2) **Stage Work :** (Class—20-30 seniors.)
　　　　　　　　(Time 40-45 minutes.)

　　Discussion and Practical Work on :
　　　　　　　　　　(i) Setting.
　　　　　　　　　　(ii) Lighting.
　　　　　　　　　　(iii) Properties.
　　　　　　　　　　(iv) Costume and Make-up.

(3) **The Play :**　　(Whole school.　80-90 minutes.)
　　　　　　　　　　(i) Brief Summary of (2).
　　　　　　　　　　(ii) Performance of " The Dumb and the Blind " by Harold Chapin.

Appendix D

The Century Theatre's Venues and Repertoire, 1952–7

From 1952 to 1957 the Century Theatre toured the following venues with the plays listed below.

Venues:

Accrington, Altrincham, Ashton-in-Makerfield, Birkenhead, Bodicote, Bolton, Blackburn, Bridgenorth, Burnley, Burton upon Trent, Bury, Bromsgrove, Cannock, Chester, Cheltenham, Chipping Norton, Corby, Ellesmere Port, Flint, Gloucester, Hanley, Hinckley, Horwich, Kettering, Knutsford, Leek, Leicester, Leyland, Lichfield, Macclesfield, Much Wenlock, Nantwich, Nelson, Newport, Northwich, Oswestry, Prescot, Preston, Rawtenstall, Redditch, Rochdale, Rugby, St Helens, Stafford, Stalybridge, Stockport, Stone, Stourbridge, Stow-on-the-Wold, Tamworth, Uttoxeter, Warwick, Wellingborough, Wellington, West Kirby, Wolverhampton, Widnes, Worcester, Wrexham.

The Company would normally stay not less than ten days in each venue and perform three plays in repertory.

Plays in Repertory:

Othello by Shakespeare
The Miser by Molière
The Sacred Flame by W Somerset Maugham
The Rose and the Ring by Thackeray
A Trip Abroad by R H Ward
The Shepherdess and the Chimney Sweep by Edward Ashley
    from the story by Hans Andersen
Flora Whiteley by R H Ward
The Mollusc by Hubert Henry Davies
A Doll's House by Ibsen
Who Cares by Leo Lehman
Mr Bolfry by James Bridie
Uncle Vanya by Chekhov
A Man of God by Gabriel Marcel
Twelfth Night by Shakespeare

Sacrifice to the Wind by André Obey
I Have Been Here Before by J B Priestley
The Father by Strindberg
The Glass Menagerie by Tennessee Williams
Christmas in the Market Place by Henri Ghéon
The Cocktail Party by T S Eliot
I Am a Camera by John van Druten
Look Back in Anger by John Osborne

Bibliography

Anderson, Michael, *Anger and Detachment* (London, Pitman, 1976)

Ansorge, Peter, *Disrupting the Spectacle* (London, Pitman, 1975)

Aston, Elaine, and Savona, George, *Theatre as Sign System* (London, Routledge, 1991)

Bartlett, C J, *A History of Post-War Britain, 1945–74* (London, Longman, 1977)

Beale, Albert, *Fifty Years of 'Peace News', 1936–86* (Peace News, 1986)

Bean, T E, 'The Compass Magicians', *Hallé Magazine* (1950), p.30

Blishen, Edward, *A Cack-handed War* (Thames and Hudson, 1972)

Blythe, Ronald, *The Age of Illusion* (Oxford University Press, 1983)

Bradby, David and McCormick, John, *People's Theatre* (London, Croom Helm, 1978)

Bradby, D, James, L, and Sharratt, B, [eds] *Performance and Politics in Popular Drama* (Cambridge University Press, 1980)

Bragg, Melvyn, 'Turn of the Century', *Punch* magazine (1983), pp.61-63

Brasch, Charles, *The Quest* (The Compass Players, 1946)

Braybrooke, Neville [ed] *T S Eliot: a Symposium for his Seventieth Birthday* (London, Rupert Hart-Davis, 1958)

Bridie, James, *Tobias and the Angel* (London, Constable, 1956)

Brook, Peter, *The Empty Space* (London, Pelican, 1969)

Browne, E Martin, *Introduction to Religious Drama* (Radius/SPCK, 1959)

Browne, E Martin, *The Making of T S Eliot's Plays* (London, Cambridge University Press, 1969)

Browne, E Martin, and Browne, H, *Two in One* (London, Cambridge University Press, 1981)

Browne, Henzie, *Pilgrim Story* (London, Frederick Muller, 1945)

Browne, Terry, *Playwright's Theatre* (London, Pitman, 1975)

Calder, Angus, *The People's War – Britain 1939–1945* (Jonathan Cape, 1986)

Chambers, Colin, *The Story of Unity Theatre* (London, Lawrence and Wishart, 1989)

Chapman, R [ed]. *Religious Drama: a Handbook for Actors and Producers* (Radius, SPCK, 1959)

Cook, Judith, *The National Theatre*, (London, Harrap, 1976)

Davies, Andrew, *Other Theatres* (London, Macmillan, 1987)

Davies, Cecil, *Theatre of Persons: Memoirs of the Adelphi Companies* (Unpublished, 1954)

Davies, Cecil, *The Adelphi Players: The Theatre of Persons* (Amsterdam, Harwood, 2001)

Dellar, Pamela [ed], *Plays without Theatres* (Highgate, 1989)

Drabble, Margaret, and Stringer, Jenny [eds], *The Concise Oxford Companion to English Literature* (Oxford, 1990)

Dukes, Ashley, *The Scene is Changed* (London, Macmillan, 1942)

Elam, Keir, *The Semiotics of Theatre and Drama* (London, Routledge, 1988)

Elder, Eleanor, *The Travelling Players* (London, Frederick Muller, 1939)

Ellis-Femor, Una, *The Frontiers of Drama* (London, Methuen, 1945)

Elsom, John, *Post-War British Theatre* (London, Routledge & Kegan Paul, 1979)

Elsom, John [ed], *Post-War British Theatre Criticism* (London, Routledge, 1981)

Esslin, Martin, *The Field of Drama* (London, Methuen, 1987)

Ghéon, Henri, *The Way of the Cross* (Dacre Press, Westminster, 1952)

Goorney, Howard and MacColl, Ewan [eds], *Agit-Prop to Theatre Workshop: Political Playscripts 1930–50* (Manchester University Press, 1986)

Griffiths, Trevor R, and Woddis, Carole [eds], *Theatre Guide* (London, Bloomsbury, 1989)

Guthrie, Tyrone, *In Various Directions* (London, Michael Joseph, 1963)

Halverson, Marvin [ed], *Religious Drama, Vol 1* (New York, Meridian Books, 1959)

Hankinson, Alan, *The Blue Box: The Story of the Century Theatre* (Melbeck Books, Bassenthwaite, 1983)

Harrison, Sarah Jane, 'The Strolling Player in British Theatre History' (unpublished dissertation, Worcester College of Higher Education, 1985)

Hartnoll, Phyllis [ed], *The Concise Oxford Companion to the Theatre* (Oxford, 1986)

Hayman, Ronald, *The Set-Up* (London, Eyre Methuen, 1973)

Hetherington, Bill, *Resisting War* (Peace Pledge Union, 1986)

Hinchliffe, Arnold P, *British Theatre 1950–70* (Oxford, Blackwell, 1974)

Hobson, Harold, *Theatre in Britain: A Personal View* (Oxford, Phaidon, 1984)

Ineson, George, *Community Journey* (London, Sheed and Ward, 1956)

Innes, Christopher, *Modern British Drama 1890–1990* (Cambridge University Press, 1992)

Jellicoe, Ann, *Community Plays* (London, Methuen, 1987)

Keily, Pamela, *Memoirs*, Hudson, Kay, and Payne, Kenneth [eds], (Smith Settle, Otley, 1986)

Kerensky, Oleg, *The New British Drama* (London, Hamish Hamilton, 1977)

Kemp, T E, 'High Adventure at Hinckley', *The Birmingham Post*, 22 February 1950

Keyssar, Helene, *Feminist Theatre* (London, Macmillan, 1984)

Klaus, Gustav, *The Literature of Labour* (Harvester Press, 1985)

Leeming, Glenda, *Poetic Drama* (Macmillan, 1989)

Lister, David, 'A nation suffering from stage fright', *The Independent*, 14 December 1993

Lucas, John [ed], *The 1930s: A Challenge to Orthodoxy* (Harvester Press, 1978)

Marshall, Norman, *The Other Theatre* (London, John Lehmann, 1947)

McGrath, John, *A Good Night Out* (London, Eyre and Methuen, 1981)

Mendelson, Edward [ed], *W H Auden and Christopher Isherwood – Plays and other Dramatic Writings by W H Auden* (London, Faber and Faber, 1989)

Murry, John Middleton, *The Necessity of Pacifism* (Jonathan Cape, 1937)

Nicholson, Stephen, J, The Portrayal of Communism and the Soviet Union in selected plays performed in Great Britain 1917–1945 (unpublished doctoral thesis, University Library Leeds, October, 1991)

Page, Malcolm, 'The Early Years at Unity', *Theatre Quarterly*, 1, (1971) 60–66

Partridge, Frances, *A Pacifist's War* (Robin Clark, 1983)

Plowman, Max, 'The Necessity of War-Resistance', *The Twentieth Century*, 5, (1933)

Read, Sylvia, and Fry, William, *Christian Theatre* (London, Eyre and Spottiswode, 1986)

Read Sylvia, and Fry, William, *Travelling by Stages* (Hutton and Shenfield Union Church Press, 1981)

Reddington, Christine, *Can Theatre Teach?* (London, Pergamon, 1983)

Rhys, E [ed], *Everyman and other old Religious Plays* (London, Dent, 1924)

Robertson, Edwin, *The Shame and the Sacrifice: the Life and Preaching of Dietrich Bonhoeffer* (London, Hodder and Stoughton, 1987)

Roose-Evans, James, *Experimental Theatre from Stanislavsky to Today* (London, Studio Vista, 1973)

Rowell, George, and Jackson, Anthony, *The Repertory Movement: A History of Regional Theatre in Britain* (Cambridge University Press, 1984)

Sidnell, Michael, *Dances of Death: The Group Theatre of London in the Thirties* (London, Faber and Faber, 1984)

Sissons, Michael, and French, Philip [eds], *Age of Austerity: 1945–51* (Oxford University Press, 1963)

Sole, M, 'Theatre in the "Forgotten" Areas', *Our Time*, November 1945, 70–71

Smart, Ninian, *The Religious Experience of Mankind* (London, Collins, 1969)

Steiner, George, *The Death of Tragedy* (London, Faber and Faber, 1974)

Taylor, John, Russell, *Anger and After* (London, Penguin, 1963)

Tolley, A P, *The Poetry of the Forties* (Routledge, 1986)

Tynan, Kenneth, *A View of the English Stage, 1944–65* (London, Methuen, 1984)

Wandor, Michelene, *Look Back in Gender* (London, Methuen, 1987)

Ward, R H, 'The Theatre of Persons', *The Adelphi* magazine (January 1941), 122–26

Ward, R H, 'A Tribunal Statement', *The Adelphi* magazine, (June 1940), 368–71

Ward, R H, 'The Hope of Liberation', *The Adelphi* magazine, (May 1940), 338–41

Ward, R H, 'What is Non-Violent Technique?', *Peace News* (1938), 5–15

Ward, R H, 'The Human Factor', *Peace News*, (1939), 8–16

Ward, R H, *Holy Family* (Adelphi Players, Ilkley, 1942)

Ward, R H, 'The Adelphi Players – A Tabloid History I', *Peace News*, 22 August 1947

Ward, R H, 'The Adelphi Players – A Tabloid History II', *Peace News*, 29 August 1947

Williams, Clifford [ed], *The Objectors* (Gibbs and Phillips, 1965)

Worth, Katherine, J, *Revolutions in Modern English Drama* (London, Bell, 1973)

Wright, Cyril, and Augarde, Tony [eds], *Peace is The Way* (Cambridge, Lutterworth, 1990)

INDEX

Ward, R.H. (Richard Heron), 1, 2, 5,
7–9, 12, 13, 18–20, 22, 25, 39, 42,
52, 53, 58–95, 102, 106, 107, 111,
113, 115, 119, 122, 143, 144, 146
Warren, The, 95, 96, 107
Waterfield, Phoebe, 28, 37, 39, 52,
65, 74, 75, 83, 113, 119, 124, 125
Way of the Cross, The, 51

White Cargo, 25
Willis, Ted, 86, 87, 137
Workers' Theatre Movement, 8–10,
21, 32

Young King, The, 33

Zeal of the House, The, 33

Other titles in the Contemporary Theatre Studies series:

Other titles in the Contemporary Theatre Studies series:

This book is part of a series. The publisher will accept continuation orders which may be cancelled at any time and which provide for automatic billing and shipping of each title in the series upon publication. Please write for details.